There Must Have Been an Angel

THE CROSS-COUNTRY ODYSSEY FROM BADWATER, DEATH VALLEY, TO THE SUMMIT OF MOUNT WHITNEY

A True Story

CWS Publishing

Copyright © 2011 Lee Bergthold
All rights reserved.
ISBN: 1463765118
ISBN-13: 9781463765118

There Must Have Been an Angel

*THE CROSS-COUNTRY ODYSSEY FROM
BADWATER, DEATH VALLEY,
TO THE SUMMIT OF MT. WHITNEY*

A true story by:

Lee Bergthold

photos by author©

Dedicated to my mother, stepmother,

father, sister, and Jerry Freeman

...their longest journey

To Wes and Paula, my son and daughter

Lee Bergthold, Founder, Director,
Center for Wilderness Studies (CWS)

Cover Design: Damian Hopper, Photoscan/Layout

Final Type/Computer: Deena Des Voigne

Final Production: createspace.com

Cover Photo: Lee Bergthold (self-timed):
    …author (right) with Jerry Freeman:
    "…we called it Nightmare Canyon,
    we thought we were trapped!"

CONTENTS

Introduction		ix
Chapter 1:	Badwater, Death Valley	1
Chapter 2:	Tule Spring, Death Valley	15
Chapter 3:	Trail Canyon, Death Valley	25
Chapter 4:	Wood Canyon, Death Valley	31
Chapter 5:	Nightmare Canyon, Death Valley	43
Chapter 6:	Northern Panamint Valley	49
Chapter 7:	Rainbow Canyon	63
Chapter 8:	Saline Valley	81
Chapter 9:	Malpais Plateau	91
Chapter 10:	Keeler Cemetery	109
Chapter 11:	Lone Pine	141
Chapter 12:	Whitney Portal	155
Chapter 13:	Outpost Meadow	175
Chapter 14:	Mt. Whitney	227
Epilogue		245

The Beginning

Most people can only imagine what Death Valley must really be like. School kids learn about such places. Writers describe early desert crossings by pioneers and gold seekers. We've all heard about the mule trains, the miners, the miles of nothing, and the humans and animals who've perished—and still do—in that mysterious land of scorching heat and endlessness.

It makes no difference what part of this vast region you happen to chance upon to understand what this 'nothingness' is all about; the ubiquitous solitude that abounds. It's an isolation that never quite turns you free, but allows you to meander at your own risk and your own leisure. But it makes no difference, no sense; you lose scale, and you drift on as if there was no ending to such a story. There is no future for such a place, only an ancient past.

Historical accounts take us back to the earliest inhabitants—distant people who roamed about when water was supposedly quite abundant. Pioneers arrived long after the waters dried to dusty sand, the desert playas having left signs that life at one time existed.

Within the past two hundred years record-keepers tell of the hardships of those early pioneers: their horses and mules;

their wagons, their dogs, their wives and kids; the hardtack biscuits, the tins of rancid lard; the mice-nibbled sacks of black and white beans along with seam-swollen wooden vats full of precious water, or half-full; nearly empty...empty!

And still, the open desert beckons.

Jerry and I knew what to expect on that October, 1989 morning. We'd spent a good part of our lives working desert and mountain. The immensity of the chore at hand—going from Badwater, Death Valley, to the top of Mt. Whitney—was a challenge we'd not take lightly. Others had crossed by road and trail, and we realized that. Sure, it could be done, but we'd do it differently. We'd lay out a 280 degree compass course, a straight, follow-the-crow line that would direct us from the lowest to the highest points in the land. It would consist of 125 miles of no roads or trails, a half-dozen mountain ranges, harsh desert, rock, heat and cold. There would be canyons, sand dunes, dry falls, and lava beds with their inscriptive fault lines and schists that epitomize the growth of time. Ancient sea beds would reflect the brilliance of age-old stars from above; wildlife would be practically non-existent unless you happened to be in the vicinity of a slush spring. But alas! Maybe there's arsenic! Non-drinkable! Where are the flies, the bees, the mosquitoes, the gnats? Look, a bird! There must be good water nearby.

But not at Badwater. That's where Jerry and I would walk away from Doyle—our checkpoint man—and Brian Bergeson, photographer-writer. We'd walk away toward the bright, white, west, toward the heart of the infamous bogs of Death Valley. We'd make our crossing at the widest point, four miles out. That would leave us four more miles to get to the other side. Total: eight miles.

Jerry hesitated, then turned back to the two men we'd leave behind.

"Here!" he yelled, while at the same time tossing a blue and red credit card back in their direction, "We won't need this!"

There was distant laughter, and even Jerry and I chuckled. He was right. Even one hundred dollar bills wouldn't be of any help where we were going.

CHAPTER 1

DAY 1

Badwater, Death Valley

You can view the bogs from atop the Panamint Range: Chloride Cliffs, Aguereberry Point, and Dante's View. It is stark enough from that perspective, but to be at ground zero—at the absolute bottom of the pan—it can be awesome!

Take a look at a map—any map, any topo.[1] What do you see? Nothing. Sterile. The breach of America: -282 feet!

Being placed on another planet would not be any more unreal compared to what we would eventually see and experience. How does one differentiate one from the other? How would we not know if it wasn't Mars or Saturn? How would we know whether or not our time machine had gone berserk? Maybe the wrong place, the wrong time.

As for this planet, it would make no difference whether it be October or not. It would never make a difference when you're in a place like the bogs. One thing for sure, if hell were

---

1   topo: topographical map(s)

to freeze over, it would be the devil himself whom you'd see roaming across those badlands.

No, no cool in such a place.

As the hours would drag by, the pit-like humidity would begin to manifest itself, sump-hole moisture drawn to a spoiling sun.

The heat itself might be tolerable to a point, but with the radiation from above combined with a reflectance from the sea bed below, the temperature would surely rise.

With one hundred degrees on our shady sides enhanced by the acres of wet mud below, the jungle-like moisture would begin inflicting its hellish venom by way of fatigue, and the ultimate, thirst!

We'd be drenched, drained, and mud-spattered, and the effects of thirst would gradually become a crucial factor in what would determine our ultimate limits.

We would spit, and it would be a combination of dirt and cotton. I would wipe my chest and marvel at the mud streaks; Jerry's shirt would soak clear through.

And water? There wouldn't be much. Two quarts each from the start.

We'd be like African dogs in a heat storm.

We kept a good distance between the two of us as we laid slack to the ropes, and my snowshoes clonked my shins as I tried to move sideways. They were sticking badly and flinging mud like a sprinter coming off the blocks. The sweat on my back was causing my pack to slide back and forth as I pulled left, then right. I wondered how long I could keep it up before the mixture of salt and dirty water—my sweat mixed with the brine of my veteran pack—would finally begin to abrade my skin. How long would I have to put up with the sting of sweat in my eyes? Yes, why couldn't it be cold?

Holding to a westerly course, we stopped on the more solid sections of ground to chip off the mixture of gravel and stucco-like muck that was jamming up our snowshoes.

We'd urinate—what little we had—then, with Jerry's binos, we'd scan the wasteland that surrounded us; there would be nothing. Absolutely nothing! It was the most barren of landscapes.

Perspiration zigzagged across the side of my face like an old trail map. I swiped at the streaks with my free hand and looked back at Jerry some sixty feet to my right. He was pulling hard on the rope as he squished, backward, into a soft spot. We were sinking in as we neared the point we'd been aiming at for weeks. It was also a point we feared: smack dab in the middle of Death Valley's salt bogs at the absolute lowest point in the western hemisphere, -282 feet below sea level.

It was at that point where lives had been lost, both man and beast, because of the thin surface crust that would give way to the muck below and take down the weight of whatever might be on top. It was a central point located in a sea bed that lay between the Amargosa and Panamint Ranges, east to west respectively. Furnace Creek Wash lay to the north, while Saratoga Springs lay to the extreme south. Those same springs were the part of the Amargosa River that would seep circuitously, underground, to the very spot where we stood—where we were sinking!

Jerry's cursing was audible, but my own thoughts were still some sixty feet away, where I had my own problems. My right leg, snowshoe and all, had just punched through. There was a stinging sensation as the brine etched at my ankle. Now, *I* was cursing!

"Tighten up, damn it!" I yelled to Jerry. "Pull!"

I pulled too, and, fighting the weight of my pack, rolled to my side to get a better view of Jerry doing the same thing at his end of the two thirty-foot lengths of rope.

"Shuuup!" My leg pulled free, but my boot damn near stayed. The scene became almost comical, except for the fact that my socks were packed with mud and sweat was flooding my eyes.

Again, Jerry jerked on the rope. The already dried mud crystals, smeared onto our backsides and lower parts of our packs—and the rope, itself—began to shoot off like miniature trinkets as we drew the rope taut and regained our footing.

"Stay with snowshoes!" Jerry yelled back as he still held pressure on the rope. He began stomping a circle within one of the whitish salt pans, sounding for a solid spot. Even at our distance, from his armpits downward, I could pick out the dark splotches where sweat drenched his already faded denim shirt.

Finally, I pulled free, but my pack felt heavier and the continued shifting was causing hot spots on my lower back and hips while, at the same time, the snowshoes still clonked at my shins with each laborious step. My toes felt cramped as I tried to adjust to the suction from below, and it suddenly became apparent that if I didn't keep my butt in high gear, I would start to sink in too. That would definitely not be a fun thing to happen, especially in a place like that.

We pulled in closer together realizing we couldn't stay in one spot too long or we'd start to sink. We unslung our packs to a ground that quivered and shook like quicksand! Like quickmud!

Jerry was still to my right and slightly behind as we moved out again, working at a slower pace, as our snowshoes clacked against the crystalline surface that resembled giant grids. Some places were softer than others, almost like sticky asphalt that you'd find on an old highway on a hot day. The shoes would flip that sticky stuff upwards, striking our upper bodies and faces.

From below the surface, the brownish ooze still continued to squeeze up through the snowshoe webbing, that reminded me of homemade pasta or, better yet, peanut butter being squished out the sides of bread.

The moisture from below was adding humidity. It was a different kind of heat. Killer heat!

We were packing supplies to be used for both heat and cold—medium-rated sleeping bags and medium-weight jackets—nothing too heavy, just heavy enough to ward off cooler weather. After all, it was October, and we were heading for the giant: the Sierra Nevada.

With sixty-pound packs and a food supply to hold us for nine days, it would be the ungodly heat and lack of water that would be our nemesis. But Jerry's brother Doyle—whom we'd just left behind—would take care of that. He would meet us at critical checkpoints to drop off water.

He'd take nothing from us, except snowshoes at the other edge of the bogs. Nor would he provide us with anything we didn't already have, except water.

"Look above!" one of us said, breaking the silence. We suddenly became aware of a change about us: an increasingly thickened sky, growing darker, as massive sky-ships of blackish-gray clouds began to build above us like smoke.

"Good gawd, maybe a cloudburst!" I said, mumbling to myself. Jerry didn't have to hear, or even answer for that matter. We both knew what a deluge could do to such a place; it'd be a death pit! We could sink clear out of sight if a ton of water cut loose.

But it was those very clouds above that made us decide on a daylight crossing in the first place. The graceful, high cloudiness of the earlier morning had given us the go-ahead without even a hint of a possible storm later on.

Yes, it would've even been cooler by night, but much more treacherous.

As it was, we struck out at dawn with a ninety-degree overcast, figuring we'd make it across the bogs by late afternoon.

We knew it would still be hot, but tolerable.

Yeah, we left because the clouds came up. It gave us a head start, and we took our water, our packs, and our snowshoes.

We'd go simple bare minimum, as little as possible. Like so many treks we'd been on before: some thirty years of backcountry travel, everything on our backs, point A to point B. No motor homes following with blinking lights, no motel-stops with cushy beds, nobody to bring us in from the rain.

Rain? Downpour?

The clouds continued to gather.

The heat wouldn't let go, wouldn't turn us loose. Isn't it amazing how the heat can make you wish for cold, and how the cold can make you wish for heat.

"Hold up, Jer!" I yelled, stopping at the same time. I was suddenly aware of the silence, and I wanted to stop and listen!

I wanted to hear more than just us yelling back and forth and the slurping and clacking of our snowshoes. I wanted to get a clearer bearing, maybe just clear my head as to what in tarnation we were doing and how *we were* doing?

We'd worked hard the past few hours and hadn't realized we were the only ones around; the only ones making noise. We were the only ones out there.

I made a motion to Jerry that I needed to stop. Dead stop!

I momentarily stood still, and, like a revolving beacon, slowly turned all the way around, full circle.

Suddenly, I felt as if I were all by myself on a vast sea, but there was no wind, no waves, and no movement, just calm.

Even though I stood there for only a few seconds, it felt much longer as the isolation of time began to engulf me like a giant flower-trap taking in a tiny fly.

It was a wonder, a strangeness. It was suddenly too hot, too heavy!

It was fortunate that we both lived on the fringes of the Mojave Desert where one hundred degree temperatures were commonplace. Jerry and I were used to heat. Still, heat is heat, and bogs are bogs, and moisture begets humidity!

The many hours, weeks, months, and years of outdoor desert living had helped us to adapt: clearing brush or cutting tumbleweeds, for example, and then hosing down under a faucet that would spew forth scalding or, at best, lukewarm water.

I whipped around quickly as a huge ball of light shafted its way across the flats! Jerry saw it too.

We noticed each other's reactions, and then, it literally dawned on us: *the sun was breaking through the clouds!*

They split open like bomb bay doors allowing streaks of sun to blast through. It glared down from a ten o'clock high, while the rays of combined moisture and light bounced and reflected like lasers. Jerry's thermometer zoomed to 110 degrees and then some. We literally cooked. We cursed, we stumbled, we wished it had rained.

But the landscape *was* changing.

The mountains we had been aiming for most of the day were suddenly much closer. We could pick out distant clumps of large brush-trees and large rock outcroppings in the distance. They weren't just mere specks like they were earlier.

But still, everything was far away.

Looking behind us—from where we started, from Badwater—it was still nothing but a vast sea of endlessness, showing only the dark outline of the Black Mountains, the closest range. It was just that, an outline. And I wondered who might be up on that high ridge looking down toward our direction. Was someone watching us, looking over us?

No human would have been up there. It would have had to been a spirit for sure. The ghost of a prospector, an Indian, an ancient man. How far back? What had this land captured in the past million years? Who was still here; who had gone before us?

Finally, we slogged into softer stuff, still falling and crunching through at several more points.

We traversed the pan's crusty edges that began to resemble swailed petri dishes with their sunken middles that would rupture into outer lips that sealed the vaults of who knows what below? How many? People, animals?

Salt grass and iodine weed appeared in small bunches at first, then more and more of the upright shoots poked skyward through the crusty surface as the last hour gave rise to even wetter ground.

The sun lay lower, direct on with a heavy glare. We had no more drinking water! But it was wet all around us as the landscape gradually transformed into a steamy dream as the sun's low, angled back-lighting forced us to squint through fogged-up sunglasses.

Then coyote tracks, some stones, and dust.

Terra firma!

We had just crossed the bogs of Death Valley.

Had we been lucky? After all, the past couple years had been dry ones. As a matter of fact, in 1969, the depression we'd just crossed had been a veritable lake. Now, with drought, the water lay below: a depressed water table, which, at best, begets mud! But we did have a surface to walk on—with snowshoes—that was the secret.

Several hours would pass, and Jerry and I would rest. We'd meet Doyle at Tule Spring for water. In the meantime, we would talk little, keeping mostly to ourselves, our own small worlds so many miles apart. And how appropriate for such a place: the isolation, the loneliness, the space a man needs for his own warrior spirit.

The sun slowly melted away, bringing down a final curtain, a final chapter. It was the ending of another day that would signal a final deadline of weeks and days clear down to the final hour of the task at hand. I reflected on a past that seemed eons ago; our planning and training, how we'd been like coaches, surreptitiously scheming and maneuvering, hoping for the greatest season ever. We were like strategists plotting last minute battle plans that would pit army against army. So it was with Jerry and me. It was us against whatever army might be out there: a compass bearing of 280 degrees, cross-country, as-the-crow-flies, dead-straight out of Badwater; crossing the bogs with snowshoes and rope; the uncharted canyons we knew nothing about; or reaching the summit of Mt. Whitney.

My thoughts cranked in on our first day out: fresh, excited, tired—all at the same time—but no big deal. This day was only one of many first days experienced by the two of us in years past. By nightfall, it'd be old hat again, and we'd begin to feel more at ease. We'd be a little tougher and, hopefully, wiser, and finally, tomorrow—our next day—everything would settle into place, a routine.

It grew dark, and I became mesmerized by a full moon that seemed to question my sanity. I wondered where Doyle had gone after Jerry and I drank as much water as we could possibly hold, being left with just two quarts each.

Doyle had left us water at the western edge of the bogs. He met with us briefly, taking our snowshoes rather than us ditching them. He took nothing else, and left us nothing but our water.

He had watched us make the crossing with binoculars, but lost us somewhere in the middle. We were a mile off course when he finally spotted us as we sloshed ashore just north of Tule Spring.

He wouldn't even camp-down with us. He'd meet us for water, then he'd be gone.

Personally, I had reservations about the fact that someone had to drop water off for us. It bothered both of us—Jerry and I.

For a good part of our lives, we had always worked as individuals, fiercely independent, mountain or desert, it made no difference. We always worked with what was available: food, water, shelter. Nobody ever helped from the outside—no firearms, no radios, no airplanes—whether we were working solo or with others. It was strange having to be checked on—in person!

But the heart of Death Valley is a bit different. There's no way on God's green earth was anyone going to cross this part of the planet without water help. Let's face it, early man followed water courses, Indians had horses to help carry supplies, early pioneers had wagons, and none of them were out to break trek records.

Early people were not out to prove themselves to the world. Nor was that the case with Jerry and me. But then, we didn't have a lifetime to follow the water courses, or the seasons, or game, or weather, moving into the mountains for the summer and then down to the lower elevations come winter.

What reason did an Indian have for climbing the highest peak? Did ancient man take time out for a marathon? Did he or, God forbid, she, head down to the local gym-cave to lift rocks after a day's foraging-hunting? Did the early settlers race across the desert for first-place in Frisco? I think not.

Those people were survivors. They had purpose. They literally had their hands full just staying alive. They risked all just going straight. They didn't have to prove anything to anybody.

Yes, Jerry and I had to have water dropped off. We wanted to come out of this alive so we could go back to our real worlds of making a living so we could do it all over again.

I thought about that often. It takes money to be poor; it takes having things so you can deprive yourself of the same. Isn't it strange how we do things in this day and age?

I stretched my legs, and from my sitting position, slipped into my only long-sleeved shirt. I shook it first, considering the fact that such a barren land does honor tiny, prehistoric, brainless creatures, that are only seen, only after they've bitten you and fled back into their minuscule dens of mud and sand. It's part of life that works best undercover, literally; they are shade and night seekers. Then there are the locust-like day flyers, the rodents, and the true spiders. And that doesn't include water, at least, not as we humans know it.

Take the spring, for instance, that lay but a hundred yards from our camp: a pool of fetid water similar to the mud-fed brine we experienced on the bogs.

The spring's water source pulsed from underneath, providing nourishment and energy to impervious, fifteen foot high wire-brush and kink-grass that would force a man to crawl at ground level to the water source, only to discover a wetness that would cool his skin, but not his gut. You could smell its heaviness, but you couldn't drink it! Wipe it on your skin and it would dry you out like a rotted pupfish. Compare that to high mountain country where you could conjure up a mountaineer's spirit; a feeling of tradition and nobility; a campfire, the comradeship, a chill in the air, a scent, cool water.

There Must Have Been an Angel

Desert is different. Its air is thick, especially with clouds. It is dry as tinder without. It's not an altitude thing. It's warm. Too warm! Not brittle, but heavy-dry. Desert nights are still and quiet, and I sat alone.

And the evening warmth, though pleasant, was but a reminder of where the day left off and what the next cycle of daylight would bring: a hot, searing heat that could deprive life from the living. It would enervate and do nothing but remind one that nighttime could be tolerable, and that daytime could be deadly. Though I fear no evil, I would fear the sun and would be reminded, constantly, that this was Death Valley and not the high country with its whispering pines and babbling brooks. None of that. None at all.

How wonderful a beer would taste, or a milkshake. I could see the frost, crunchy with tiny ice particles, like slush, and then those winters down to zero.

Korea! First Marine Division—twenty below—men froze to death.

Jerry pulled up next to the fence post where I sat. Even in the moonlight I could make out the white dust streaks that slacked his long trousers. We finished supper and laid out our sleeping bags that we constantly shook out for bugs' sake. However, we wouldn't sleep in them, only on top.

That's desert for you.

And we'd learn, later on, about a man who would attempt to cross the bogs some time after Jerry and I did.

The man died in the attempt.

Yeah, that's desert for you.

CHAPTER 2

DAY 2

Tule Spring, Death Valley

The actual 280 degree compass course we had laid out would cut across just north of Tule Spring, proper, and practically run straight up Trail Canyon. Fair enough.

We had arranged with Doyle the night before to meet up with him later that night, or at least the morning after, in Wood Canyon, which was up and over the crest of the Panamint Range.

And so it was on that second day.

There was no such thing as sleeping in, not on this kind of desert anyway. With the low-slung Funeral Mountains due east of us, there would be no way the sun could hold back. The minute it would crack through the lowest point, our tolerable nighttime air would dissipate into nowhere.

Yes, it became just plain hot as we loaded up. During and after our meager breakfast of an apple, plus twenty almonds each, we did little complaining about having to abide by a cardinal rule: little or no water, little or no food. What food you did have would be as water-succulent as possible. You'd pack it early and deep inside your pack, which was then insulated by wrapped-up clothing.

Jerry and I clasped one hand each, like a high-five, for our own private and silent prayer, which, understandably, coincided with the final load-up chore of cinching down water bottles to our packs. We'd constantly check each other's load for the sake of those bottles. We called it prayer. It was prayer all right—water prayer! Oh, such a precious cargo.

With that, and the realization that nothing would really be downhill from that point on, we began to drift away from the Westside Valley Road that skirted the western flank of the salt flats—or bogs—in a northwesterly direction toward Trail Canyon, the huge opening that lay ahead. We'd hold that course until midday.

It would take that long to reach, and actually enter, that broad, alluvial opening where the terrain would become steeper and rougher. No, we weren't on desert sand, but rock and chunks of eroded strata that were like cement before the sand and gravel was added, or maybe it had rained, and maybe that caused it all to solidify.

It was typical of cross-country travel—that being without trail or road—and clumps of starched brush began to make their debut.

By midday, we huddled in on the stone side of an earthen pinnacle that reminded me of an ant hole, upside down. It was coarse and rounded, it gave quarter shade. We had lunch—an orange a piece. It was the honor system as far as the water went, literally. I was already near the end of my first bottle; Jerry was into his second.

We didn't talk about water. It was like two men on a life raft, each plugging a leak at opposite ends of the raft. We had to depend on each other, to a point. But what if one man drank, or lost, his water? Does the other offer his? Do you murder the other man so you wind up with four quarts? Do you want to carry four quarts? On the other hand, what if you wind up by yourself and need help?

Imaginations play tricks.

We ate our oranges.

The rest of the day was hot, steep, and rocky with very little sign of a supposed map road that went up and into the heart of the canyon. At times, we thought we had the road, or remnants thereof. Mostly, it was just walk-work on an unstable surface that slowly transformed into rock and boulder, scree and talus.

We would separate from one another by flanking side-by-side, but still staying in visual contact. People need space; they need time to think. We had both. More importantly, two persons working the flanks would simply cover more area. In other words, you see double, and you convey the information—"… what's out in your sector?"—to one another.

Looking for shade—any shade—became priority. Straight-up-and-down, midday sun didn't offer much in the shade department; it didn't offer anything, except a relentless heat. At the opening of Trail Canyon, the reflected sun, especially during the morning hours, angled off the snow-white salt bogs, which, at that point, lay some eight hundred feet below us. As the sun arched higher overhead, during its twenty-four hour sojourn, the foil-like reflections would wane, but direct heat would become more intense as the sun would arch at high noon. All that morning, the heat that funneled itself up the mouth of the canyon would be stored in the earth and rock that we trod upon. We were literally walking on a giant solar slab.

Finally, with a late afternoon sun that conjoined with an eroded and rock-strewn canyon wall, shadows began to manifest themselves as shade.

We worked in close to some of the more deeply etched clefts and rested in the welcome shadows. We even dug in sandy spots for possible water, knowing full well that if we weren't careful in doing so, we'd burn up critical energy stores and create even more body heat.

Then, we did begin to talk about water.

Jerry had been in that canyon before, in 1987, when he did the same trek, but not the same route as we were doing.

He attempted to cross the bogs during the night; he punched through, and fearing for his life, retreated and circumvented the entire bog area. He eventually wound up in Trail Canyon, and he remembered a spring.

Even the map showed a spring. That spring just had to be up there! But the year had been dry.

We began to talk about water again.

Dark. Moon up. Must rest. Must eat.

We must've been close to the 4,000 foot elevation mark, and still the night was warm, but to the point of almost being comfortable.

The night before had been too warm. Not that we minded that, but it made us uneasy knowing that if it was that warm at night, what would daybreak bring?

It didn't disappoint us.

Even though the new night was pleasant, we were again, uneasy. Very uneasy. It was past dark; we were under moonlight, and still hadn't found the spring. We finally stopped.

We should've been there—and we were—but we were keyed up and concerned.

Damn it! We couldn't even eat! And it could've been such a super night: mild temperature, big meal, tired as hell. We could get some sleep. But no, none of that. We had no water! Or I should say, I had maybe a cup left; but at that point, what good was that going to do?

We laid out our sleeping bags, and yes, we did have supper. We split a friggin' cucumber.

We didn't talk. We just sat and thought; sat and crunched—and savored—our half of a cucumber.

I began to feel like a fool. There we were in a remote canyon, far from anybody. We were far from Doyle, way too far. We were behind, but, damn, it had gotten real steep. Why were we continuing on when we didn't even know for sure what the water situation was like? We should have been heading east toward Furnace Creek, anywhere but where we were.

But, then, how do you ever know what's ahead? Do we need a radio? A weather check? An altimeter? Radar? A lawyer in case we stub our toes?

Hell no we don't! This is crazy, but it's not! You've done this too many times. Yeah, I know, but not without water; am I stone, am I clay?

"See you in the morning," Jerry finally said, as he lay back on top of his open sleeping bag.

"You mean you're going to sleep? You haven't even taken off your boots. How can you relax like that?" I said. I was talking just to hear myself.

"Great supper," I continued, "I'm gaining weight."
Jerry laughed.
I laughed too. Good sign.
"Yeah, see you in the morning."
But I couldn't sleep.
Fifteen minutes past.
"Jerry, Jerry, you asleep?"
"No."

There was silence. I stared up at the moon. I looked over toward Jerry who was leaning up on one elbow. He had his slouch hat on.

"Why don't we head on," he drawled. "We're not even tired."

"You're right, we're exhausted! But let's get the hell going, let's march to the moon."

By flashlight, Jerry's watch read midnight. Even without his light, we could still read the watch face, the moon was that bright. The rocks, the canyon walls, and the bushes were like tombstones, and we were wandering in a strange place. At first I thought of a cemetery. *No, too morbid, too dramatic. This place is beautiful, you lie!*

Several hours of moving further up the canyon, and we still hadn't located the spring.

Dead on our feet, but not accepting it, we trudged along. Then, with spurts of energy, we'd strike out toward a side chute chasing a moonlit shiny spot only to find shale, white rock serpentine, or just a slick piece of granite embedded vertically in the side of the canyon wall, situated at just the right slant to catch the moonlight. Dead end!

Then I realized something new. Jerry's speech had become slurred. But in our present frames of mind, whose speech was slurred?

I rambled on with Jerry; the conversation was really with myself, Jerry was the sounding board. I had the feeling he really didn't want to hear me and wanted me to shut up, but I didn't. The more I talked, the less he'd answer, and the more concerned I became. I talked even more, but he didn't sound like the coherent Jerry I was used to hearing.

We stopped.

"Let me see the light," I said. Jerry handed me the one flashlight we were using. We'd use only one at a time, and even then, only occasionally. The moon was doing most of our work.

But I didn't have to use the light. Suddenly, I became aware of tiny cobwebs stretching between Jerry's lips. In fact, the moonlight was even more effective than the flashlight; the mucous had an eerie irradiance to it. Like a dentist's headgear, the stringy bands of spittle spread from his upper to lower lip. It was like cotton candy.

"Shit!" I muttered in a raspy hoarseness, and, at the same time, dropped down hard and slid out of my pack. Quickly, I undid my water bottle and thrust it into Jerry's chest.

"Here! Rinse your mouth, then swallow!"

"I'm okay," he drawled.

"Damn it! Drink it! It's only a swallow, kill it!"

I stretched my own lips, feeling for the same thing: cobwebs, thirst, a thick mouth.

I brought my fingers up to feel. I did so, ever so lightly, so as to alert my senses. I wanted to be acutely aware.

Yeah, they were dry and smooth, no moisture.

I quickly licked them, like blinking my eyes. Everything seemed to be okay, but, like a medical student observing the illness of others, I, too, was becoming paranoid.

I quickly knelt down in front of Jerry, who was already sitting on a large rock.

"Listen, Jerry," I said in the same hoarse whisper. "You stay put, I'm going to check this place out. I'll leave my pack here, I'll leave the flashlight. I can see okay."

We were at a point-opening on a supposed roadbed. It was beginning to circle from a due west position to a new direction of southwest. I left Jerry and headed in that direction.

The moon had crept further west, and as it continued its arch-like curve, the resultant shadows began to stretch into longer ribbons of dark.

The tombstones of an hour earlier were now oversized sabers and spears that grew even more ominous as I worked my way toward the east side of the shadowy canyon.

I then turned west, bearing in on the moon that angled toward me. In that fashion, the moonlight would strike the road on a rebound. I wanted to stay out of the shadows as much as possible and keep the moon's light reflection out front.

I was looking for something very specific.

Suddenly, I thought I saw it. No, just a shadow.

I hurried to the next one, the next, the next, the next. Damn shadows!

I relaxed and quit chasing. I sat, briefly, then continued on, but by then, I was stepping over the shadows instead of on them. *You're not going to fool me, Mr. Moon, not me!*

To really settle the score, I would step down extra hard onto the next shadow that came up.

And I did!

Whoops!

I turned quickly and, regaining my footing, jammed my boot toe back into the dark spot.

I slipped!

Dropping to all fours, I quickly, but carefully, brought my hand down over the shadow and onto it.

It squished!

It was soft; it was wet!

Moving on my hands and knees like a wrestler, I shifted right, right up to the edge of a thicket. I shifted again, moving my body from right to left so as to keep myself on the shiny side of the moon strike. There, before me, at the edge of the brush, the gleam of wet earth manifested itself.

I had found water!

Jerry and I followed the tiny feeder of water to a small cave-like overhang. There, the water was seeping out of the rock wall into a small pool of cool water. Cool, cool water!

We drank, we relished, we ate, and we finally slept.

Words simply can't justify our feelings at that moment of discovery. It was as if all of life's burdens were suddenly lifted; it was like going to heaven, and I can only speculate on that.

Were we there? Heaven?

Only we knew.

CHAPTER 3

DAY 3

Trail Canyon, Death Valley

The morning was beautiful, and why shouldn't it have been? We had slept, we'd had food, and we had water. What more could we have asked for except for the fact that we had missed joining up with Doyle the night before. Obviously, best laid plans do go awry.

But long-term plans were not particularly in our thoughts at that moment as we slumbered, half-in and half-out of our sleeping bags, in the almost cool of the dawn's early light.

We had made camp on the west side of the water-cave canyon wall, which gave us an early shade. The sun would slowly rise behind us, behind the wall. It would find us soon enough, but for a brief interlude we'd relish the comfort of the soft-blue shadows.

Slowly at first, we rose to the occasion: re-rolling bags, pads, and space blankets; re-packing food and clothing; recoiling ropes; and jamming stuff bags, knives, spoons and frying pans.

We drank water, then loaded up our two-quart bottles, each. It would be another day.

With our own portions of half-cups of granola, powdered milk, water, and, then, another cup of boiled noodles, the Peak-1® stove and extra fuel canisters were finally packed away.

We greeted the new day with eagerness, realizing that all we had to do was finish climbing to the top of the ridge and then drop down to the other side: Wood Canyon, Doyle, and more water!

Reluctant to leave our water cave, but anxious to move on, we started up the road that we had finally located the night before.

In less than an hour, tucked away to our south side—and we could've easily missed it—we came upon the unexpected: the ruins of an old mining town.

It was the brownish hulk of an old truck hood that first caught our eye. It stuck up like a bench mark, as if some surveyor had used it as a reference point, or maybe it guided a prospector finding his way in the dark, like using moonlight to find a spring, yes!

Moving to our left, and through the brush, we caught sight of distant piles of rubble that resembled prairie dog hills; hills that were nothing more than rotted metal, tons of it.

Tons of brown and rusting scrap lay about like wounded dinosaurs, like solar panels sucking up strength from a blast furnace sun.

As we passed the first mounds and came up over a small rise, we realized that we'd come upon a ghost town. We were witness to a burial ground of man's past.

Hulks of old cars and trucks and machinery lay scattered about: gears, cams, axles, cable, refrigerators, swamp coolers, and piles of cans. They would eventually—perhaps, in a thousand years—revert to dust, like rock wearing to sand.

The millions of pieces of scattered glass looked almost like chips of obsidian, or mica, or feldspar—fool's gold—if the sun's light hit just right when we moved or changed our positions in relation to the angle of the sun. It was the same light, the same gold sparkle that, in the past, had beckoned those who'd tried their luck with the earth, the picks and shovels of a past era of men, women, and children. And how many of those human souls had it taken to create such a place? How many souls were still there?

Over the years, I had learned about spirits that would roam from shack to shack, cave to cave. Strange beings that seemed to only move about at night, visiting yesteryear's mine shafts, outbuildings, sheds, and barns. Rarely, would those beings be seen or felt during the day or in open vistas, plains, or mountains, unless those places were where people had lived and died.

It was daytime now as Jerry and I rummaged through the debris. We were free to roam. Nighttime might be different.

Dropping our packs, we circled the camp in opposite directions. In less than an hour, we met, full circle, at what appeared to be a store front. Inside, there was a table and a chest of drawers, old hinges and latches, and finally, an inscription of some sort that was written on the back of a piece of old wallpaper. It seemed to be a grocery list, and it was dated early 1950's. Not old by ghost town standards, but nonetheless, a partial clue as to what might have been.

Our full-load packs felt heavier than ever as we got ready to continue. We had pushed ourselves hard the day and night before—harder than we realized, but with rest, water and food, we had renewed energy and felt relief. There's always a downside of starting all over again—another day.

Finally, near the crest of the Panamint Range, we rested in what seemed to be a man-made, or 'dozer-made' cut in a lower portion of the steep, craggy wall we were working. The road—what was left of it—finally gave out near the top, and a burro-run picked up where the road disappeared. This gave us all the trail we had to have, as it led, precariously, to the top of the ridge.

Being in a more neutral environment—no bogs or raw, sand-like desert—and being higher up in elevation, our water supply wasn't nearly so critical. At half-a-day, we were one bottle down, each. Not bad.

We felt exuberant as we lipped the last remaining chunk of ridge, and were finally able to look out over Wood Canyon.

In celebration, we sipped water and gave high-fives, even though, in the direction we were heading, there was still nothing more than desert.

And Wood Canyon? It was a level-sloping valley that curved, gently, from north to south, like a giant Pyrex® bowl. No trees, no woods, no canyon! Just a pock-marked earth with strewn-about, lava-like scree. The pea-sized gravel would eventually disintegrate into smaller and smaller particles—deep sand and dust—which would gradually transform into spongy earth, with age-old plant life that probably looked dull green from ten thousand feet above.

Pilots would wonder.

Doyle was ecstatic in finally sighting us as we drifted into view some twenty hours overdue. It was also obvious that he was concerned: he thought he'd missed us somehow, and he suddenly realized the awesome responsibility that had been unavoidably thrust upon him. Even Jerry and I hadn't realized what the effect would be, but suddenly, the immensity of it all began to hit home. Sure, there were the bogs we crossed, but that was done with. We now found ourselves in a totally new set of circumstances: farther and farther away from civilization, and water, and the real possibility of missing Doyle at a checkpoint.

The meeting was an exciting one, but it was a short coming together. "How you doing?" "Good job," that sort of thing. Then, we re-checked compass bearings, and almost religious-like, performed the most important task of all: drinking as much water as we could hold, while at the same time, filling our quart canisters to the brim.

We took nothing else from Doyle, gave nothing in return.

Then, without fanfare, Doyle simply drove away.

How vivid that memory is: Jerry and I watching the blue Toyota® drift farther and farther away. We were entranced as that metal and plastic, motorized box bumped its way down the rutted dirt road. We watched the ghostly images created and illuminated by the Toyota's red taillights: small dusty rings of puffers each time Doyle hit the brakes or a bump. Jerry and I watched this strange scenario in silence—until the truck totally disappeared into the darkness.

Seeing Doyle for even a brief period of time seemed unreal. His truck was totally out of place, out of era—a total incongruity. It was as if our conscience showed up, just briefly, to remind us of the fact that we were jeopardizing our very souls by what we were attempting. Nobody really had to say anything, we knew, we all knew. We'd all meet, exchange bits of wisdom about the desert, coordinate compass bearings, drink, fill our water bottles, then Doyle would be gone.

It wasn't the bogs, or the isolation; there was something mysteriously different about everything—the lack of water! That's how Doyle fit in. He's the one who did all the waiting, the wondering, and the worrying. He really did have the water. He could save our lives! He had to follow the right compass bearing in order to be at the correct checkpoint. He had the water. *He had the water!*

Jerry and I began to worship Doyle.

CHAPTER 4

DAY 4

Wood Canyon, Death Valley

There was no hiding the sun the next morning. One minute it was open shade, then bright light, nothing in between. However, one thing was significantly different and welcome. It was cool. Cool enough, in fact, for us to slip into our Patagonia® shells, to thwart a wispy breeze blowing east to west down the canyon from the Panamint Ridge and beyond.

There was a dry crispiness to the 5,000 foot level where we laid down our sleeping bags, and where Doyle had left us water the day and night before. He had waited until he was convinced he'd missed us, and had even driven up-canyon as far as he could in hopes of finding us. During his brief absence, he left a big bottle of water on a rock pile with an American flag taped to the bottle in case Jerry and I would come onto it while he was gone. It all turned out well, however, as that's where the three of us eventually came together, right there at the bottle with the American flag. Even though Jerry and I were overdue, and Doyle was obviously concerned, we had made it to our checkpoint just like we planned. Jerry and I drank our precious water from Doyle, filled our canteens, and then Doyle left, drifting away into the distance.

Jerry and I moved out of Wood Canyon with caution. Doyle claimed he heard snakes during the day and evening before while he waited at the checkpoint, scanning the terrain with binoculars, and hoping to sight our two figures somewhere along the skyline. "They rattled and stretched," he said, "They're setting up camp!" We chuckled and chortled at that, but Jerry and I decided to take no chances when we broke camp. We split up our tent poles between the two of us, each of us extending our halves into beater sticks to beat the brush as we headed out over the scrubby plateau. We wanted to warn any snakes that we were coming through.

In spite of a breeze, and by the time we dipped into a large, dry creek bed, the desert sun was relentless. Even snakes stayed out of the direct sunlight.

We dismantled the beater sticks and fell into our regular routine, and because we had nothing better to do, we made a pact: we'd not talk about water, or snakes, or scorpions, or spiders, we just wouldn't talk for a while.

We headed west, through Emigrant Canyon, hoping to cross at a point just south of Pinto Peak. Without difficulty, we found that location on our topos, but after that, the maps didn't offer much information. It was as if we'd struck a vital nerve, and we were probing into strange and secret places. It even seemed as though the cartographers were confused as the flatland lines seemed to squiggle into little canyon off-shoots that led to tighter and tighter lines, which, in turn, meant tighter and tighter canyons. Perhaps, the map makers figured nobody would go into those sacred places. Why worry about accuracy if nobody knows better? Just make marks, make it look good, who'll know?

One canyon after another, no names, just lines, tiny turbulent lines like cramped-up snakes. It was Zebriskie Point a dozen times over. A soda cracker would've read better, or if one happens to subscribe to a pin-the-tail-on-the-donkey mentality, you might, by chance, luck out.

"Look! Nova!" We discovered a landmark.

"Piece a cake," one of us quipped.

"Screw it! Let's get it on!" and we refolded the maps and checked each others' packs to make sure everything was secure. We headed west, toward the next range.

For several hours we made our way over the eastern flank of a gentle upgrade. The brush turned from pure desert flora to a low alpine growth that indicated we were definitely gaining altitude. The flat rock surface, or tiles, lay snug in their grouted positions as if gelled into place by some liquefaction of years past, centuries of blowing wind with sand and rain mixed in, centuries of heat and intense light, centuries of earthquakes and shifting plates underground.

We lost ourselves in our private languid thoughts; we drifted apart at times, catching sight of one another at a distance, while always knowing where the other was.

We took a half-hour lunch break: nothing salty, no water. Save it, just a swallow or two.

We continued, and by three in the afternoon we were climbing a sloping summit. We looked westward, and, for once, the land didn't really look quite as sinister. We were actually moving through some scrub pine and cedar—squatty bush-like plant life that resembled small trees. We felt good. For the first time in several days, we began to feel as though things were shifting in our favor.

"Piece of cake," one would say.

"What was that? Piece of cake?"

We were cautious with each other in regard to those euphoric feelings. We'd both spent years doing wild-assed-treks, and were leery of suddenly being half-way comfortable. We teetered on the edge of almost being suspicious, not of ourselves, or of each other, but of the land.

Like I'd always told people I'd guided for: "...become complacent, and it'll sure as hell turn on you. Learn to be comfortable, to be at ease, to be confident, but be aware, be cautious!"

Jerry rechecked our compass bearings. We kept going, actually moving downhill, slightly off the other side of the summit. As our pace quickened, we began to feel better about our day's work. We followed the gradual contour of the small valley we'd dropped into; it eventually funneled into another sandy creek bed.

We stopped. We both sensed something wasn't right, something was amiss. We leaned our packs against one another then urinated. That was almost a joke—no water, no pee, or very little. We laughed nervously and kicked at small rocks like high-strung schoolboys. It was obvious, we knew what was wrong. There was no trash! No cigarette butts, no foam cups, no beer cans, no glass, no shell casings, and no tire tracks! No footprints!! Nobody!!! Nothing!!!!

Another hour and a half passed. It was late afternoon. Roughly three hundred yards ahead was a large rock overhang that allowed the creek bed to circumvent its base. Beyond the rock was sky!

We joked about how the beautiful, surrounding landscape was going to change, abruptly, as we rounded the rock. How the earth was going to drop off into nowhere, a bottomless chasm where monsters would be waiting with boiling cauldrons at the ready.

We continued joking, talking and laughing at our make-believe scenario as we moved in closer to the rocky point. Our legs had readjusted to the downhill grade, and we shifted our weight as the sandy surface squished beneath our feet.

We got closer. We grew silent.

We approached the rock. We made the turn!

We stopped dead in our tracks.

Our fairy tale was real. The earth did drop off—I mean, *it dropped off!*

We had walked in from a high-desert, cedar-strewn plateau that looked like a Sierra Club backdrop right onto an overlook that plummeted into purgatory. After all these years, we should have known better.

Reality snapped in. We'd made a mistake. Mistake? No, just gotten too cocky. We'd seen this sort of thing many times before in the backcountry. This was no different. It was like a Marine patrol: too easy, too quiet!

We couldn't afford mistakes.

We clicked back to our old selves. There was work to do. We had to get down that cliff. As far as we could see, left to right and north to south, the plateau simply broke off, etching out a deep canyon below.

It was a flip-flop scenario of the mighty Sierra Nevada Range that gradually tilted upward from the San Joaquin Valley, then eastward to the Owens Valley. This range was just the opposite. Looking from east to west, from the rock point of view, the land fractured and convulsed into an ancient abyss, the kind we joked about an hour earlier.

It was approaching dark by the time we set foot at the bottom of the cliff. It was indeed a chasm, with an east wall that looked like dime-store rocks that'd been dumped into a dirty fish bowl—dried, brown mud and clay columns dribbled straight up and down like rusted gun barrels.

The sun disappeared, the walls became darker and darker as we finally took a rest and sipped some water. We looked back toward the direction we had just slid down, hoping we wouldn't have to go back up.

The gun-barreled walls became more ominous as the canyon became another shade darker. We were silent as we cinched into our worn, sweat-dried, salty, dusty packs. Jerry's face was lined with smudged sweat marks. I rubbed a grimy hand over my chin stubble. It wasn't the dark we were afraid of, nor the canyon itself. No. Just water! How long would it be before we'd see Doyle again? How far can we go into that canyon? What if we had to come back out? Who'd know?

"Welcome to Nova," mumbled Jerry.

"Screw Nova," I exclaimed. "Too scary for Nova. How about Spook Canyon?"

We weren't surprised at finding no prints or tracks in that canyon: human, animal, or otherwise. We continued to expect this in the days to follow. We accepted the fact that we were in no-water country and that we'd have to continue westward in order to find Doyle. We were in land so wild and primitive that it seemed that mapmakers had long since given it back to the cave dwellers.

My thoughts rambled:

It's like turning off all the noise that you've grown accustomed to over the years. How enlightening to be in such a strange and intriguing place; so far out of the way that nobody knows about it. Nobody wants to go there. Nobody can survive there. We only hear of places where our vehicles will take us; we seldom hear of those places where so little is known.

Author Edward Abbey once said: "We need wilderness whether or not we ever set foot in it. We need a refuge even though we may never go there."[2] *But Jerry and I were there. We understood Abbey's words completely.*

The canyon narrowed, the sun was gone, and the walls closed in. We continued downhill. The sand deepened and the dark thickened.

---

2 Desert Solitude by Edward Abbey, Random House Publishing Group, Ballantine, New York: 1985.

We passed many side canyons, but didn't take the time to investigate, we couldn't take the time. We had to go as far as we could before it was pitch dark.

With each new bend, our forward passageway became narrower. We grew extra alert and cautious and more suspicious with the downhill slope. It was too easy!

The sweat on our faces had dried, and our packs were less sticky. A cool breeze soothed our adrenaline-spiked bodies, keyed high from a day's work and the excitement generated by the exploration of such an unknown Disneyland.

We passed more offshoot canyons, and, in almost total darkness, could barely see the crinkly details of cliffs that drew us into the arms of Dracula. We could make out huge pockmarks, like bat caves nestled in between cathedral-like spires or Roman candle bursts frozen in time. We could see the convoluted skyline—a row of blackened teeth. The entire mass must have dried too quickly as it poured over the crest, the jagged holes a result of an imaginary planetary law of beginning-earth's gravity.

Jerry stopped. I bumped into him. We both stared upward.

"Like being inside a dried-up volcano," Jerry said somberly.

"Let's get outta here," I replied, knowing full well I was just making sounds, just to hear myself. "Let's get the hell outta here!"

But we didn't move. We just stared upward. We knew we weren't inside a volcano—or were we? We knew we could get out. Well, could we? When? How?

The walls couldn't hurt us unless they came tumbling down. No, it was water we were concerned about. Always water. But we weren't talking about water, snakes, or scorpions. We were talking *canyon*!

"Let's get going. Last place in the world I'd want to be during a flood or earthquake," I added.

We continued, knowing full well that the canyon would have to end eventually. They all do, but it still wasn't beyond sensible reason to feel like we were suddenly trapped. Feelings like that are not unusual; they're paramount. A signal that goes off in the human mind. Something that cautions man, or beast, into readiness. Ready for what? Being trapped? Cornered?

We'd play it cool. We'd backtrack if need be, that is, if we didn't go too far in, and if we still had enough water to support such an emergency plan.

We rounded more curves, peering briefly into ubiquitous, sinister-looking side canyons. The further we went, the spookier everything became.

We curved several more times, knowing we'd have to stop soon and make camp. It was totally dark.

We rounded right, and stumbled onto a drop-off. We couldn't see the bottom!

"This is it," one of us mumbled. "This is it!"

We said nothing more. We didn't want to know what we thought we already knew. We just didn't want to know anything right then. We knew we couldn't see the bottom. We couldn't see the top anymore either. We were in the middle.

Dropping our packs, and automatically leaning them against the base wall, we fumbled for flashlights. Silently, cautiously, we edged our way to the lip of the drop-off. Our beams barely showed the bottom.

"Dry fall," Jerry whispered sternly. "Plug. Eighty, maybe one hundred feet down."

I chuckled. Not ha-ha-like, but matter-of-factly, "So? You take right; I'll go left. Check it out."

I grabbed Jerry's arm and beamed my light into his face. He squinted, but there was a look of confidence on his face. I was glad to see it.

"Go easy," I said, "Go easy."

Jerry chuckled, as we separated into the darkness.

We explored as best we could, using our flashlights. We yelled back and forth, then finally returned to our start-stop point.

"We're boxed in!" one of us said.

"We camp, look again in the morning."

"Agree."

We settled down for the night.

I'm not sure what time it was when I awoke; I rarely have to get up during the night, even to urinate. This is especially true when fluid intake is below normal. I rolled off the top of my sleeping bag. It was too warm to be zipped up inside. As I walked away from the rock overhang where we were sleeping, I began unzipping my trousers then my work shorts underneath. I stopped. I stood, waiting. I didn't have to urinate, but it was the only justifiable reason for being up.

I was about to make at least a half-christening, when suddenly, a dark-skinned snake-like creature stuck its head out from between my legs, from inside my shorts! I jumped back. The snake made a low, hissing sound. I backed against the rock wall. Then, with added shock, I noticed that my feet *weren't feet after all.* They were strange looking lizards! Large, scaly ones with dark green coloring that resembled a hideous scum, the kind you might find on stagnant water.

I turned quickly and tried to run, but the wall stopped me. From up-canyon, a huge, prehistoric beast-bird swooped down. It looked as if it had simply dropped off from the cliff above, from the saw-toothed ridge that must give birth to such monsters. Its spread-out wings were like mighty animal nets, or chutes used to engulf prey. There were curved hooks in its scalloped wing tips that were of the same repulsive green color as my lizard feet.

"Jerry! Jerry!" I called, and turned just in time to see him *pouring* the last of his water onto the sand. It, too, was green....

Like a shot, I sat up, damn near hitting my head on the overhang. I let out a long sigh.

"What's the matter?" Jerry asked as he rolled to his side. His sleeping bag made a rustling sound like wings.

"Can't sleep," I replied. "Can't sleep. I hate canyons like this."

"Yeah, know what you mean."

Jerry wasn't sleeping well either. Our mutual concern about getting out of such a canyon subliminally echoed between the two of us as if some telepathic force was at work.

"I've been dreaming," I continued. "Weird dreams, nightmares!"

And *we were* concerned! The last thing we wanted to know before ending the day was that maybe we were at a plugged dead-end. Trapped! Would we have enough water to work our way back out? Enough for a day and night to get back to where we last saw Doyle? But Doyle wouldn't be there. Besides, we hadn't planned on backing up. We'd tried to consider all eventualities, but it was impossible to cover everything. Any fool knows that, and it's the fool who gets trapped!

Finally, I really did get up. I walked to the spot where the beast-bird had been. I looked up at the ridgeline, half-ass expecting to see the same monster. I unzipped my trousers, and my shorts. I was okay. My feet were okay; it was just a bad dream.

"Just can't sleep," I repeated to Jerry as I walked back. "Canyons like this give me the creeps."

We both knew the danger of sleeping where we were in the case of heavy rain. Choices come hard at times. We both knew what earthquakes could do, so we had purposely slept, or tried to sleep, under a rock lip that would divert anything coming down from the top. But what about the other side? Our exposed side. Such sweet choices.

Propping my flashlight on the rock ledge beside me, I wrote in my notebook:

"Somewhere to our northwest two men died in a place called Dolomite Canyon. We knew there were others who had died out there too, but we didn't talk about it much since we had our own problems. We had our own private canyon to worry about. By the topos, we thought it was Nova, then we changed the name to Spook! By tomorrow morning, we'll be calling this place Nightmare!"

CHAPTER 5

DAY 5

Nightmare Canyon, Death Valley

Dawn:
We packed up. Even though the sunlight was indirect, we marveled at how daylight can be such a phenomenon.

Jerry took the right side, the cliff side. I took the left. Fifteen minutes later, Jerry yelled. First, he'd caught a tarantula using his shirt as a makeshift net. It escaped. Good omen. Second, there was no way out along the cliff side. Bad omen!

Scrambling on hands and knees, I found a way across a medium-level ridge. The scree slide was bad, but I was going somewhere.

We joined and cautiously began to figure out where we could and couldn't purchase foot and handholds. Whereas I can out-endure Jerry on long, straight-out, hard climbs, especially at altitude, and better tolerate heat on my bare skin and go farther with less water, it's Jerry who excels at footwork. I mean fancy footwork. He's dazzling when it comes to working points and high cliffs.

I'll get there okay, but I've admitted to Jerry that fear creeps in. I slow down and begin to think. I see and feel the danger. Jerry then becomes the pivot man. I swear, he can stand one-legged on a twenty foot pinnacle and spin like a gyro. That man sticks to walls like a fly. I respect that. He's not a big man. He's shorter than me, stocky, and tough!

As we inched our way across the ledge that led to nowhere, it was one of those scary times: straight up and down on the north side, yet we had to proceed. Behind us was Nightmare, ahead was Doyle and water. We had no choice.

Cautiously, we finger-tipped our way toward a larger rock. A foothold first, then one handhold. We'd try and keep two points down at all times, three points are better.

Jerry worked ahead. He saw a way, a slot down through some jagged rocks that, for once, looked like doable granite instead of the lava-pocked, Swiss-cheese rock of the canyon we were climbing out of.

"Rope!" Jerry yelled, excitedly. "We can do it with rope!"

I edged up and looked over. "Yeah," I said, lazily. Lazily? It looked crazy wild!

"Yeah, okay. I'll do it. I don't like it, but I'll do it. *We'll* do it!"

We laid out one thirty-foot length of rope, looping it around one of the granite spires that was to be our safety. It was a procedure we had used many times before.

We dropped our packs at the ledge, supporting them with smaller rocks and stones. Then, we bodied ourselves down through the bigger rocks below. We also secured the packs with a rope end.

Half-way down, I locked-in while Jerry worked down to a lower level. With the rope, I lowered the packs, one by one. Jerry anchored up for me as I followed, then we pulled the rope down to us.

We locked onto one another, wrist-to-wrist when necessary, then worked inch-by-inch across the rock's natural strata, making damn sure we weren't trapping ourselves. We made progress.

We finally rested on a small ledge to re-coil and repack the rope and bandage one of Jerry's rock-cut fingers. I had literally followed his blood trail from the top of the ridge down, and I jibed him about marking up the rocks and how we should've at least taken time out to do some decent rock art.

We laughed, genuinely. We were excited, and the blood jokes were a welcome relief.

The excitement wasn't just about a cut finger. We were getting down and out, we were leaving Nightmare Canyon!

We proceeded the rest of the way across the ridge, then lipped a second one. That put us between a hard place and sky. One more hump and we could see our way out. A steep downhill slide, a broad wash.

We worked our way across the broad, deep-sand wash, then up over a smaller, though steeper hill, then down through some scraggly brush and rock, below, on the north side.

After another fifty yards and a side canyon, we both suddenly heard it—a swooshing sound like a car going by.

By gawd, it was!

Above us and ahead was a road, a real, live highway. It was the highway that led up to Towne Pass—the highway that came up from Panamint Springs. We couldn't actually see the road because it was above us, but as we got closer, we could make out the asphalt berm. We saw something else—the top of Doyle's truck! We had hit our checkpoint right on target!

We shouted!

A head popped up over the berm near the rear of the truck. *It was Doyle!*

We stood around the back of Doyle's truck drinking water. We were keyed-up, we walked in small circles, talking all the while. Then we'd be silent. It was difficult to explain to Doyle what we had just seen and been through: total euphoria, total excitement, and total accomplishment. Not catastrophic—no, far from it. We were honored to have been the guests of Nightmare Canyon. It honored us. Then Doyle told us about the earthquake the evening before—San Francisco, October 17, 1989.

We knew then why the night had been so strange and wild.

Yes, Nightmare Canyon.

We said goodbye to Doyle about eleven in the morning then Jerry and I dropped over the west side of the highway. The area was steep and strewn with large granite boulders. Once at the bottom, it leveled off into another broad wash that meandered lazily toward the south and then west.

Panamint Springs was roughly ten miles ahead, by road. We'd never see the place. No, we'd stick to the open desert, cross-country, continuing on our 280 degree compass course.

The heat began its incessant return. Coming down from roughly 5,000 feet (our last camp) to about 1,500 feet brought the return of one-hundred-degree-plus temps. It was back to the same desert, the same starch, the same dry, the same heat-ridden canyons that Death Valley is so noted for, especially the infamous ones like Dolomite Canyon.

Finally, we actually crossed the mouth of Dolomite Canyon, which is known as a deadly place to be in since two men had died there a few years back. They had hiked into the heart of the chasm, then lowered themselves by rope, into a deep chute, only to come upon a deeper cut. The latter drop-off was deeper than they could handle, and, having pulled their rope down after they got to the bottom, they couldn't retreat to where they dropped down from originally. They were trapped between two dry-falls, or plugs.

Yes, trapped. Yes, dead!

Jerry and I finally came upon a deep, earthen, east-west ledge where the four o'clock sun provided shadow and shade. We took it. We needed the rest.

Scat from wild burros was evident, and it was fresh, real fresh. We probably ran the beasts off by our approach. We felt sorry about that, but we needed the place. We needed the shade, the rest. After a late lunch, we lay in the burro pits and slept.

Once we'd left, the burros would return. We only borrowed the place. We were drifters, squatters. We could survive only by moving on. They would survive by staying.

It was near dusk and still very warm. We were at 1,500-feet elevation on the northern stretch of the Panamint Valley. The ground beneath us was as solid as brick, and in the distance we sighted what looked like small, square buildings. Moving closer, we saw they were car bodies, old car bodies: rusted, bullet-ridden hulks that resembled giant tin cans.

They would be our home for the night.

CHAPTER 6

DAY 6

Northern Panamint Valley

It was an eerie setting. There we were, in the middle of a dry, wide open lake bed, camped next to a couple of rotting car bodies where the dim early morning light offered its own view of a prehistoric montage. How many times had the sun risen and set on this piece of earth? How strange it was that the discarded bodies represented nothing more than seedlings gasping for life in a barren desertscape that gauges its age by millennia.

It was symbolic, a paradox. Lake beds mean water, but this one was different. It offered a hard, whitish-tan, brick-like surface. If we had brooms or sails, we could have swept across such a mighty space like desert witches on a gigantic lunar plate, our own alien hiding place.

It was nothing like the bogs.

That land was like a stage, it was a testament to the physical likeness of all mankind—past and present. How long would it take for this desert to die? Would it ever? How long would it take for old, rusted metal boxes to completely rot away? And what about Jerry and me? If we should die there, would our bodies return to dust? Did that mean we would return to earth? Were we treading on the remains of the many that were here before us?

It was one of those kinds of mornings.

Jerry looked so out of place in his puffy, sky-blue sleeping bag superimposed against the rusted hulks behind him. North Face® would be proud.

He slept as I tied my boots. I wanted to be up early enough to photograph this particular camp. I wanted to capture Jerry sleeping next to the old cars. I wanted the photos to show how incongruent everything was. The autos did not belong there. On the other hand, I suppose we didn't belong there either.

Once Jerry woke up, the cars took on a new meaning. They represented civilization. We leaned our packs against their metal sides and cooked a meager breakfast using the bullet-ridden walls as a shield. We were in good company; other human beings had been there before us.

It was one of those mornings.

It wasn't long before Jerry sighted Doyle's truck heading our way.

"Here comes the water truck!" he shouted as he tracked Doyle's progress with his binoculars. "He'll have no problem finding us out here. Hell, it's like an airstrip!"

It was like an airstrip: flat, level, and solid. The main highway heading toward Panamint Springs was maybe five miles away to our south. Panamint Dunes and Hunter Mountain were to the north and Rainbow Canyon was to our west.

Rainbow Canyon? We hadn't decided on that yet. That canyon could be a major obstacle, and our 280 degree compass course put us right down the middle of it. Do we go through or around?

For days beforehand, we'd studied the topo maps to get a more accurate bearing on whether or not it would be possible to go up Rainbow. If we did, could we get out at the end?

A flyover report by retired Air Force Major David Brands was not at all encouraging: "Does not look good; maybe go around, bypass Rainbow!"

Highway 190 traverses the southern lip of the canyon. I've often wondered and marveled at the sight, by car. It's a mini Grand Canyon, yet, you never hear about the place.

Looking over the terraced gorge by road, there are only a few places where you can actually see the canyon floor. The canyon drops away abruptly some 1,500 feet. It's very much like the Grand Canyon on a much smaller scale, but just as impressive.

The multi-colored impregnated rock walls reflect a rainbow likeness when viewed from lip to lip, or edge to edge. Even Doyle was impressed while driving past, "Hell yeah, it's a rainbow, but you're not gonna catch me trying to get to the end of it! That's one hell of a crevice, a deep rugged one. You got your work cut out for you if you do go in."

It's difficult to get near the edge, for a look down the side, as the ground is uneven and gravelly. Millions of tiny lava pebbles dot the hardened surface. If you step too close to the edge you'll lose your footing. There's nothing to hold or hang onto once you've lost it. There are no hand or foot rails, no safety snaps or swivels, and definitely no sidewalks.

But there is one place where you can look over and see at least partway down. At about five hundred to eight hundred feet, there are the remains of a fairly new truck, just barely visible. It's never been reclaimed. You can't get to it from the top or the bottom—it, too, will stay 'til it rots.

Earlier that morning, Doyle proclaimed that Jerry and I looked like hell, which convinced us he was onto something. We laughed and eventually confessed we did miss being able to bathe—how sweet it would've been. A simple garden hose with cold water would have been welcome. However, we didn't want to take a chance asking Doyle for additional water. The water supply Doyle carried was for the *three* of us, not just for Jerry and me. That was a major consideration.

It wasn't a simple matter for Doyle to get gas, food, water, or to even make phone calls. He'd already driven several hundred miles to restock his own basic supplies while manning checkpoints and getting water for Jerry and me. We began to consider some of the consequences of our expectations of Doyle.

Suppose he is ten, fifteen, or fifty miles out in the middle of nowhere and his truck breaks down? That's the problem with motorized vehicles these days, especially in places like where we were. It's not the vehicle's fault, but the drivers who take their vehicles to the limit. Sure, the vehicle can take you in for miles, but can you get out if there's a failure?

Just because Doyle carried water didn't mean he did so without a price. Try getting to a phone out there, or finding gas and food. Indeed, there were many things to consider.

We'd worry about a bath another time.

Rainbow loomed ahead. We agreed: we'd go through and worry about the other end when we got there.

Doyle had long since left, leaving Jerry and me our two quarts of water, each, and our own task at hand: the crossing of the northern flank of the Panamint Valley and on toward Rainbow Canyon.

And what a canyon it was! It stretched, majestically, across the western skyline, not as a huge hunk of mountain, but as an indentation that loomed above our line of sight simply because we were on a lower level of 1,500 feet elevation. Its size, alone, was taking on an ominous distinction, and by the time we finally reached the alluvial entranceway into the mouth of the canyon, its ominousness was warranted.

With this broad and sprawling landscape before us, we soon realized that we really did have our work cut out for us. There was a very good possibility we'd not reach the far head of the canyon by nightfall.

Even though we were now out of the heart of Death Valley proper, the harshness of the flats remained business as usual. Our lower level elevation still gave us temperatures in the high nineties, which increased, considerably, because of the reflective surface we were walking over, and the fact that we were moving at a faster pace because of the unobstructed and smooth surface.

But we couldn't waste time on the flats; it was a race with the sun! Simply put: no shade! No shelter!

We moved quickly, we laid down some miles. Our faster pace and hotter bodies required more water. That was always a trade-off. By midday, when we crossed the valley and began to work our way into the actual basin, we'd already taken down a quart of water each.

The ground surface was level until we entered the canyon, and the pitch gradually increased. The ground turned rough almost immediately as the canyon floor gave way to eroded ground-cuts. None of it was soft; it was still solid. Even the rocks, large and small, were firmly embedded in the dried and broken surface.

Our first priority, once inside the canyon, was to head for the southern bluff that would eventually transform into the canyon's left wall. We were hunting shade, and we needed rest. We finally found relief, but our location was precarious.

The canyon was still quite wide, though it was closing in rapidly. As we continued on, our depth and distance perception became increasingly distorted.

Finally, we declared the place a chasm. We could no longer tell exactly where we were in relation to the top sky-wall.

The place was different from Nightmare, where we simply had to move forward to get out. With Rainbow, we knew there was a road above, a highway that skirted along the top and near the end. Doyle would be in that area, most likely at a large turnout called Father Crowley Point. It's in that general area where you can look over the side and see the remains of the wrecked truck below. This is the place where Jerry and I would climb out, if possible.

With our present location, Doyle wouldn't be able to see the bottom of the canyon—or us. Likewise, we wouldn't be able to see Doyle.

Regardless, we planned on moving forward until we would finally reach the end of Rainbow. We also realized that reaching our destination would not be possible until the next day, as the day's shadows were drawing longer and deeper. We'd surely know when we were at the end point, because the canyon would simply close out and we'd literally hit the wall!

We rested in deep shade and ate a late lunch. We drank little water realizing that it might be a while before we would see Doyle again.

Uncertainty began to manifest itself once more. Would we have enough water to back out if we couldn't climb out at the end? Could we even get to the end? Were there plugs we don't know about? Dry falls?

At the last Buick® Camp checkpoint on the valley floor, we discussed all those options with Doyle. If we couldn't get out at the end, we'd retreat to the mouth of Rainbow and probably head for the highway. It would be a long haul.

Once again, we began to worry about water. Without it, there wasn't going to be much of a supper.

We moved like plow horses following a setting sun. It was pulling us, beckoning: "Just a little farther, a little farther."

The canyon air finally began to cool us, somewhat, the funneled walls closed in even tighter.

The sun continued to fade, playing its final hide-and-seek with the southern wall. Then, the shadows were complete.

During our next break, I put on long trousers and a thermal sweatshirt. Jerry put on a lightweight wind shell.

The shade, the shadow, the cool, what a relief.

The canyon curved and twisted, and the floor became more and more like a river bottom: sandy with all sizes of boulders strewn about and brush growing haphazardly where you'd least expect it.

I was slightly ahead of Jerry when we came upon a large truck tire and wheel half-buried in the sand. Another hundred yards and we came upon a second set. In both cases, the tires were still inflated, but the roughened metal wheels and rims looked old and worn.

Finding such oddities in isolated country ordinarily would have been the source of much excitement. But being in the vicinity of a road at the top of the cliff, we summarized that the junkers had been pushed over the side for the thrill of seeing such monsters tumble to the depths below. Can you imagine what a sight that must have been? How about the abandoned truck lodged halfway down? Accident or intentional?

These discoveries were significant! They were an indication that we were nearing the head of the canyon. We were further into the belly of the whale than we realized.

Father Crowley Point was near the head of the canyon where the highway skirted at its closest point. This was the most logical place to push something over the edge. If that were the case, we were near the end. Judging from the half-buried composure of both finds, we speculated the wheels were thrust over several years ago. Heavy rains, cloudburst, what have you, occurred time and time again, washing the wheels west to east, downstream in our direction.

There we sat, sipping water, pondering this newfound revolutionary evidence. It was relief! Something new added to our day. Let's face it, what does one do on a tiny island in the middle of nowhere on a Saturday night? One extrapolates the profundities of wheel-wash!

The fact of the matter is, we were actually laughing, and having one hell of a good time.

"Tell me, my dear Watson," chided Jerry, "according to the carbon dating on this here wheel…"

"Oh crap, Jerry. Just figure X equals Y and the dammed things just floated down!"

"Yeah, but you gotta figure air pressure."

"You mean, like some idiot just floated on down, shot the rapids, hit a few speed bumps, and wound up right here at this very spot?" I was half-laughing and slowly nodding my head in disbelief.

"Sure," Jerry continued, "little rough comin' over the top, but then it levels off."

We laughed aloud, urinated, walked in small circles, stared at the walls, looked upstream then down, and sat some more.

I held my water bottle up to the almost dark sky and watched the liquid swirl at the halfway mark. It was suddenly quiet. The party was over. We headed on.

But our party wasn't over!

I was still ahead of Jerry when he yelled, "Yo, look here!"

I wheeled around to see Jerry, maybe fifty feet behind me, staring down at the ground.

"You missed this!" he said, excitedly, and pointed to the ground. "Look!"

Hustling to his side, we both looked in amazement.

"Damp sand!" I muttered, hoarsely, in astonishment. "Damp sand!"

In double fell-swoops we slid out of our packs, dropped to all fours, and began to dig.

"Dig, dig, dig!" we chimed, and we did! The sand got wetter and wetter, and then we hit bedrock.

"Rock!" said Jerry, in between breaths.

"Keep digging!" I shouted. "We'll get through!" We extended the ends of the hole. "Feel for a lip," I continued, "a break, fracture, chip, anything. Damn! There's water here!"

Finally, at my end of the enlarged hole, probably a foot down, my fingers caught a lip.

I pulled. The rock came loose. I gave a mighty tug, and the rock barely cleared the hole.

"Stand back! Maybe a geyser!" I yelped as I rolled backward with the rock in my lap, laughing all the while.

"We hit it! We hit it!" we shouted. The rock was soaking wet underneath.

We slapped and grabbed each other's shirtsleeves in celebration, like pseudo high-fives.

"Okay, okay! Let it settle. Let it settle."

On our hands and knees, we watched as the hole began to fill with liquid.

I swear, if anybody could have recorded that crazy scene, it was like a fairy tale—schoolboys shooting marbles, men digging for gold, or thirsty men digging for water.

Yes siree, it was there! We continued to watch the hole as it filled. Brown water!

Our excitement ebbed, and we settled back into a routine. We expanded the hole and lined it with small rocks as best we could. Then, we waited. Waited for the small chamber to fill, then to settle.

Gradually, the dark brown water turned to a coffee-and-cream color, and without waiting forever, I tested the first drink with a shot in a film-canister.

"Hmmm, hmmm. Mighty fine. Like wine in the summertime."

I passed the next to Jerry.

"Just like Sparkletts®. I mean *just like Sparkletts!*" he sang. I thought he was trying to sell the stuff.

He continued, "You know that brown rice pack we've been carrying? The one you have to add water to?"

Jerry didn't have to say anymore.

While we continued expanding our water hole, the sun made its final descent. We barely noticed. Suddenly, we were getting out flashlights. We had to shut down for the night and find a place for sleeping.

"Right here," said Jerry. "Right here next to the hole."

"No!" I replied, seriously. "Too low. We have to get higher up, but still close. If we should get rain in here, we'd catch it, big time."

Jerry knew that as well as me. Wild rain in the desert can be treacherous, especially if it comes in a cloudburst. On the other hand, there wasn't a cloud in the sky; I'm just too damn cautious, but then again, that's what keeps two men alive. One covers the other's fallibility; we don't argue about it. We respect that in each other.

We both feared complacency; we knew what it could do. Play by nature's rules, we both knew that.

We moved up-canyon another hundred yards and settled for a spot that was on a large level shelf, roughly ten feet above the actual canyon floor. If renegade water was to cut loose from a distant storm, we'd have a chance to scramble higher up. It wasn't level at the next steppe, but we'd be able to cling to rim rock until the high water receded.

In any case, we set camp. Our dinner? You guessed it—brown rice with brown water. Who'd know the difference?

In total darkness, except for the light from our flashlights and from our Peak-1 stove, we allowed our morale to soar as we unwound from the day's labor, exalted by the fact that we had water not too far away, and that we had dinner made possible by that very fact.

If digging for water wasn't the highlight of the day, what happened next surely was. An occurrence so unplanned, so coincidental, so lucky, one had to believe that someone, or *something*, must surely have been watching over two men cast asunder into the wilderness.

Halfway through dinner, Jerry jumped up, and yelled, "Look! A planet!"

It happened so quickly, I almost spilled my frying pan full of rice (cooked with brown water), God forbid! By the time I regained my balance from being sprawled about, Jerry was standing upright, looking toward the southwest sky.

"Where?" I blurted back.

"There. Look. Look! Look at that light!"

Jerry was blocking my view. I shifted left and I saw it. Yes, there was a light. A very bright light. It was far away, but it had to be a powerful one for us to see it that clearly, regardless of the distance.

"It's Doyle!" exclaimed Jerry, in total awe. He then whispered, "It's Doyle."

"How in the world?" I drawled, not finishing. I, too, stood in awe.

And for a second, it sounded like someone calling down to us, but we couldn't make it out.

"Is that God calling?" asked Jerry. The serious tone of his voice brought us both to out loud laughter. For me, it was the deadpan delivery; for Jerry, he just blurted it out without thinking.

During all the commotion, we retrieved our flashlights and shined them, blinking, toward the big light. It flashed back.

It had to be Doyle!

And speak of coincidence: we find water at point A and camp at point B. Doyle evidently roamed around, topside, where he was manning the next checkpoint. It just happened, *just* happened, mind you, that he caught a glimpse of our small flashlight beams down below through a slot opening that enabled him to see all the way to the canyon's floor—a one-thousand-to-one shot!

So, he rigs up a big spotlight onto his truck and flashes the beam down toward us.

Pure conjecture on our part, but then, who else could it be? *It had to be Doyle.*

Jerry and I were ecstatic. We had water, we had food, and we knew where we were, and Doyle was waiting for us at the top.

Everything was working—well, except for one thing. How do we get out of the canyon?

Tomorrow morning, we'd find out.

CHAPTER 7

DAY 7

Rainbow Canyon

Daybreak.

First thing we did was re-spot the point where Jerry saw the "planet" from the night before. Sure enough, at the very top of the cliff, in a tiny V-slot catching the early morning sun, was a figure standing upright, waving his arms, up and down, like a big bird ready for takeoff.

"It's Doyle, alright," said Jerry calmly, as he watched through his glasses. "It's him, damned if it isn't. Looks like a toy soldier up there." Jerry sounded and looked like a field commander surveying the battlefield.

"Wait 'til the water man sees that brown stuff you got in your bottle," I quipped.

"Yeah, if we can't get to him, we may be drinking that stuff on the way outta here, or all the way back."

"I hear you," I said glumly, understanding the truth of the matter.

Once again, we fell silent. Doyle was suddenly another matter as we shifted into our own private thoughts, our own meditation. We would pack without fanfare, our minds consumed with one thought: how do we get out of the canyon?

The instinct for survival seems to manifest itself in way of mixed feelings and deadpan composure. It's part of the overall process of adaptation of fight or flight. It's a preparation for any eventuality, much akin to the warrior about to face an unknown enemy, the athlete about to perform before thousands, or a man about to face a personal challenge emotionally and physically.

The challenges and stresses of modern society are not what I speak of (i.e., telephones, computers, meetings, TV, radio, cars, freeways, deadlines, and so forth). I speak of the basics: Where do I sleep this night? Where is my food, my water? How do I protect myself? Your enemy is the natural world that surrounds you.

There is a difference.

It's a primitive experience that stimulates, a stress that kindles a fire in the belly, a burning desire to succeed, to survive.

Jerry opted to work the middle south wall; I would work clear up to the head, to the actual box-end of the canyon. Jerry's route looked like the only possible way out, but the end had to be checked, regardless. After an hour's reconnaissance, it was obvious that Jerry's route was the only passage out, and that, in itself, was not without doubt.

The end was simply impossible: straight-up-and-down cliffs and a giant granite bowl that resembled a mighty shaft without its cover. It was nothing but acres of solid rock that curved like a huge wheel, like one of the wheels we discovered early on, but much larger by comparison.

In addition to being old and worn, the end of the canyon was etched with watermarks that stained the vertical cutouts of ancient waterways. It was top to bottom dry falls; plunging dry-water trails that intersected with the wild, horizontal patterns of contoured color. It was a once-in-a-lifetime experience, the end of the rainbow!

Jerry started up first: the pivot man at work.

We would switchback as much as possible and with each oblique cut we would pick up elevation. We'd work it slow and thorough. After all, we were staring at 1,500 feet, bottom to top!

From the start, we tested every footing and made sure of our handholds. Whereas the end of the canyon was solid granite, this area was loose with unstable rotten rock. Nonetheless, it would be secure enough if we just took our time and made sure of every move.

It wasn't a totally vertical wall, but terraced in such a way that it would shoot off straight, then there would be a tiny level space, or a natural. It would shoot off again, following the strata, then end in nowhere, and we'd have to hunt and search for a better route.

As we neared a pinnacled ridge, at roughly a third of the way up, the pitch increased dramatically. Jerry went right, and around, and out of my line of sight. I took a shortcut and went over the top of the jagged outcropping. I lost a handhold when a small, top spire broke off in my right hand. I gasped audibly and instinctively gripped up with my left hand. I then turned and looked back down toward the floor of the canyon, a mistake!

You fool! Never look back, never look down!

I recouped quickly with a new grip. I took on a different spire. I tested first. I tugged, and it held!

Pulling myself up, I swung around and above the main spire, and Jerry came back into view. He was working horizontally, left to right, from my position. He looked back toward me, and I gave an everything-is-okay wave. He kept going until he was blocked off.

While he searched for a new way up, I shot for a slot slightly above me. It worked. Now, Jerry was below me.

This system worked well for our two-man approach. We simply watched one another and capitalized on each of our block-ups. In other words, when I saw Jerry come to an end and he couldn't proceed, there was no reason for me to initiate the same maneuver in the same direction or location. Likewise with Jerry. He would take signals from me.

Three-quarters of the way up we finally met on a small ledge. We took a rest. There was even room to slide in with our packs.

We were warming up. The day's temperature was on the rise, along with our body heat, despite the fact that the sun would probably never strike that portion of the wall, ever!

At least one thing was for sure: we each had a quart of beautiful, brown water. Enough for a try at the wall, enough if we had to go back down. If that were the case, we'd simply go back to our watering hole and fill up with two quarts each. That should be enough water for a retreat to the highway, if need be.

In that respect, we felt confident. We had our bases covered.

We continued. Even though we were thrust in close to the canyon wall, and couldn't—and didn't—expect to see anything of Doyle, we felt we were heading in the general direction. Obviously, we were heading up; how far from the Point and Doyle was anybody's guess.

Nearing the last section, we worked closer to one another as the possible routes became much more limited. The wall became considerably steeper, until suddenly we were confronted with narrow chutes, or funnel-like corridors, that required wrist-to-wrist, push-and-tug assists from each other. We took turns going first, or ahead, until finally we ran out of options.

And yet, going back down wasn't even discussed. In fact, going back down would have been worse! Rock climbers know this well; work yourself into—and through—a difficult section, and then try the reverse. Sometimes it's impossible! Going up, you can see where you're headed, where your steps are. Going down, you don't have the same perspective. Jerry and I were well aware of that fact, well aware of trapping ourselves.

Finally, we had to stop to critically analyze the situation. And yeah, we looked down.

"Woe is me," I thought, vividly, when I saw where we'd come from. "No way we're going back down this thing," I mused. "No way!"

So, up we went. Somehow, we kept finding footholds and places to grab onto. It became, literally, one step—inches—at a time.

There was one minor slip. I jammed back against Jerry. "Push!" I yelped. "Push against my pack!"

He did, and I took a new purchase. I locked in, then turned and pulled him in behind me. We came to a stop, on a narrow ledge, so narrow that we both had to change positions at the same time.

We turned left and headed up to the next outcrop. One would push, the other would pull. We'd turn left, and Jerry would lead; we'd go right, then I'd take the lead.

And that's how we lipped the final yards of Rainbow's south wall, the final fifty feet, then thirty feet, and finally we knew we had it!

"Go, go, go!" we shouted to one another, like brother athletes at the finish line.

Adrenaline surged; we were kicking in! We were almost there!

"Go, go, go!"

We kicked into smaller rocks that churned dirt into dust. We afforded ourselves that careless luxury since we were then side by side rather than beneath one another to catch a rock in the chops. No, we were actually scrambling side by side, coming up over the top!

"Go! Yo!"

Suddenly the sky opened up, the sunshine rushed down upon us, and we caught sight of Doyle running up-and-down on the next rolling knoll over.

Yes, it was Doyle, yelling his head off, bounding our way, while at the same time trying to maintain his footing in the loose scree.

"Whooo-weee!" we shouted. Doyle shouted likewise.

Trying to get traction on the uneven surface, we moved as fast as we could toward Doyle.

We came together, high-fives and all.

We were all at the top, together, and at the end of Rainbow Canyon.

"...our seventh day...sixty-some-odd miles over rough terrain travel...Rainbow Canyon, halfway point to Sierra Nevada Range and to Mt. Whitney...."

I closed my journal and walked over to Jerry and Doyle who were still talking excitedly about brown water versus 'Doyle water,' the next checkpoint, map coordinates, and so forth.

We were all excited about having made it that far. It was like a Labor Day celebration as we drank and toasted fresh water, told stories, and finally laughed about the planet episode from the night before, and how Doyle picked us off with his spotlight.

The party was brief, however, as we settled back into a more sedate mind-set: preparation for the next crossing, the next checkpoint.

I sat down next to a rock to rest. Not a rest, per se, but I suddenly needed time to reflect. I saw this in Jerry, too, as he laid out the maps on the flat ground. He lay down next to them, not for a better vantage point, but for his chance to stretch. He, too, needed to catch up with himself.

We lulled in the late morning sunshine, and it suddenly dawned on me—us—that the sun's rays weren't blazing hot like the days before, they were almost soothing.

Like the night I sat under a yellow-blue moon at Tule Spring after crossing the bogs—seven days ago—I needed to mentally calculate and analyze what we were doing. I needed purpose.

Seven days. Sixty miles. We had expected to reach Whitney in eight or nine days. If Rainbow was to be our half-way point; seven days, doubled, gave us fourteen, just a wee-bit off.

Our food supply was set for eight days, with a re-supply at Lone Pine, a full-sized town west of where we were on Highway

395. That would be our last major crossing before hitting the Sierras. Lone Pine was at least three days away. It was going to be close in regard to food. We weren't going to take anything additional from Doyle. Water, okay. Food, no!

Like all the treks over the past thirty years, everything we needed would be carried on our backs for whatever situation we'd encounter. Lone Pine was suddenly a major factor in the overall scheme of things. Once there, we would resupply, just as any Indian, pioneer, settler, or wagon master would.

The food is critical in more ways than one. It's much more than a balance of basic nutrients plus carbo, protein, and fat, but at what juncture are these components needed? At what point do you really energize the troops? What's the weather like? Hot? Cold? How do you prepare and preserve? Freeze-dried? Powdered? Fresh? Canned?

And for desert crossing—the hottest weather—the dependency on water begets a certain diet: apples, oranges, bell peppers, carrots, squash, and cucumbers. Yes, we carry and pack such perishables even in hot weather. They are packed first thing in the morning—deep inside and center-packed—wrapped in clothing. The most fragile are eaten first, the tougher ones later. Those foods give you juice, fiber—and water!

Other staples would supplement: nuts, rice, gravy, pancakes, dried fruit, even potatoes and onions. Most important, whether it be hot or cold: *garlic!* Raw garlic! Big doses!

Worried about water that's safe to drink? Splash any water you find across a flat rock, and smell. If it smells like rotten eggs, forget it! No life in or about your water source? Forget it! If you do drink—like, brown water— then add plenty of garlic to your meals: this lily family herb is considered antiparasitic, antiprotozoic!

During the winter of 1963, while traveling cross-country by bicycle (Fresno, California to El Paso, Texas, 2,700 miles in thirty-one days) my buddy and I almost starved. From sunup to sundown we rode. We lost weight, we needed more food; water was secondary, our energy expenditure far exceeded our caloric intake. All I thought about was fried chicken and chocolate cake!

I dozed. I watched Jerry next to the maps. He had lost weight, I had lost weight. Why the hell was I so hungry all of a sudden?

I'll tell you why. The weather was getting cooler. Water wasn't so critical, we were thinking more about food than we were about water.

Brown water, brown rice. I dozed, I dozed.

We had completed our mighty climb out of Rainbow Canyon; we reveled and basked in the sweet glory of success. But, from the emotional and physical high, there would surely be a payback. It was, therefore, understandable that the grade leading away from the canyon would seem like twice the work of days before. We had drained ourselves. Not just from the 1,500 foot climb, but from the high demands of the past seven days.

There's a term that exemplifies the sum total of such demand: *hitting the wall!* Jerry and I finally hit that wall on the seventh day.

It wasn't a matter of not being physically in shape. Jerry and I were both dedicated to hard work, and the conditioning we involved ourselves in was patterned into a lifestyle that required day-in and day-out conditioning—year 'round—it was a given.

If we hadn't been in shape, we would have hit that proverbial wall much sooner. We wouldn't have even left Badwater in the first place. No, this kind of venture takes total commitment, physically and emotionally. It's not something that kicks in overnight. One prepares for months and years.

We headed out along the Santa Rosa Wash that meandered west to east. Its origination was the millions of acres that spread westward, and eventually included the watershed of the southern portion of the Saline Valley. In considering this enormous spread of badland, one could soon extrapolate the horrendous consequence of heavy rain: water rushing across, around, and beyond. The rivulets, the tributaries, the streams, and the creeks that would eventually funnel their fury into the upper reaches of Rainbow Canyon via the Santa Rosa Wash.

What must it be like to be in that canyon when all that water would begin to build and spill: Nightmare Canyon, Dolomite, Nova, any and all the canyons in that vast desert.

What does one see? Look at the eroded, cracker-like mountains that expose their pachyderm-like hides. Nothing grows: serpentine, talc, shale, lava, belch stone, sand, dust, solidified earth, soil cement. It was a sandpaper planet.

The water comes in torrents. No forest here to soften the deluge. It comes and goes, another hour and thirst returns.

It was only a matter of an hour or so, and our bodies and minds began to adjust to the reality of what we were involved in. It all began to ring true when the terrain offered itself up as being halfway hospitable.

The abrupt landscape began to transform into rolling levels of sage columns and arroyos that, when peaked, even offered a view of the distant west: more desert, some flats, and another mountain range, the Inyo, dead ahead! But something else! Look! The stimulus needed to bring our senses all the way around *did* happen.

We spied a glittering in the distance at some two hundred yards. The late afternoon was the right time of day—a westerly direction—going against the low-setting sun. Within those given parameters, anything of glass or metal substance that lay upon the exposed surface would give us a reflection.

It was akin to scavenging a sandy beach: pick a windy day and walk against a lowering sun and against the wind. Two things happen: the wind causes lost coins to turn upright—on end—while the backlit sun makes them sparkle, or reflect.

Now, on the desert, we followed a course toward the glitter, from two different directions.

All of a sudden, there it was on the ground, right before us.

"Good gawd, look at this!" Jerry said. "Ammunition!"

It was confined to our immediate location, though we imagined the debris as being everywhere, everywhere we couldn't see. It must be scattered all around, we thought, and it was military! After all, during World War II, the military trained extensively throughout the desert southwest.

"It's Patton!" said Jerry, half-way serious, but joking, nonetheless.

"Be serious. It probably was," I retorted. "The Desert Fox—Rommel!"

"From a secret underground base at Badwater, home of dog fish and assholes that explore by night and hide by day."

We laughed.

"No, no, no. Pupfish," I said. "Main staple for armies crossing the desert."

We made light of the matter, and then began to seriously analyze the legitimacy of what we were seeing.

I made notes:

"...50-caliber ammunition, some lying loose, others still attached to what looks like broken, or pulled apart, bandoleers...broken, like forced, or maybe collision? Explosion?"

We found some empty casings, some with the actual bullet head loose with exposed powder inside the casing.

Our discovery conjured up memories of a solo trip I took several years ago. While in a high desert area, I came upon the canopy of an aircraft that presumably was from a Korean War vintage jet. I foolishly picked up a tubelike device that was laying alongside the canopy. Much to my chagrin, it was full of explosives; it looked to me like it was an old fishing rod tube.

Fool, fool, fool! I thought of myself then. I thought it again with the ammunition—beware!

I took pictures while Jerry wrapped up several empty ammo rounds to put in his pack. We'd turn the items over to military ordnance people later—we planned to return someday (which we did) to recover the items that most likely dropped off a half-track or tank, or might have been dropped from aircraft. We would never know.

We finally crossed the Darwin Plateau as the sun set lower on the horizon. It sank slowly while still piercing its way over the Inyos, to the west. We lowered our heads to escape the straight-on glare; the air was still, though the heat was gone.

The sun offered one last blaze as it slid behind the distant range. It grew suddenly cooler as dusk began to spread its deep-shadowed wings. The fire-sun of Death Valley had lost its chance at capturing the two men—us! Jerry and I had broken from the clutches of the notorious desert's reputation.

We continued to study the horizon, a much easier chore since the mighty sun was out of our direct line of sight.

We trudged along in a slightly northwest direction, stopping only to pull on warmer clothes, including caps and even balaclavas.

This was the first time we had to even *think* of headgear. The weather was changing; it wasn't just cooler, it was cold!

A slight wind stirred from the direction we were traveling. It made noise against our capped ears, and like animals, it made us extra alert and restless.

The dark, too, made us more cautious, since we saved our flashlights until we really needed them. Even though the ground surface became much more unstable because of poor vision, we still kept the lights off.

Finally, we saw what we were looking for:

"There he is," I said, not too excitedly and without breaking stride.

"Right on target," replied Jerry.

It was Doyle, still miles ahead, but right where he was supposed to be. This was not going to be a difficult checkpoint. Jerry and Doyle had worked out the crossing of 280 degrees, placing Doyle at the Saline Valley Road. All Jerry and I had to do was aim dead-on. Doyle was there. We could see his big light in the distance.

"Hey! Gimme a Lite!" I quipped to Jerry, and I momentarily imagined myself actually downing a Bud Lite® beer.

"Here! Have a Lite!" and Jerry picked up a rock and tossed it my way.

I jumped with glee: "Good gawd, mutiny!"

The rock cracked—granite to granite!

Finally, because of the darkness, we were forced to break out our flashlights. We flashed signals in Doyle's direction and then shut the lights down to conserve batteries. Doyle didn't respond.

We stumbled into more rocks and brush, and, once again, we had to break policy. Lights came and went, and every once in a while we signaled Doyle. He finally responded. He saw our light; we saw his.

Suddenly—almost instinctively—I reached out and grabbed Jerry by his pack. We stopped.

"Smell!" I said. We stood, silent. "Hair conditioner, like wash on a line on a windy day. Smell it?"

Jerry took in a long draw. "Yeah, yeah, I think I do."

"I'd bet a dollar to a donut that there's a woman out there. Doyle sure as hell doesn't smell like that!"

Jerry chuckled, "You got that right!"

We continued, and the 'scent of women' got stronger.

"Hey, Jerry." We stopped again. "I'm serious. It smells like women!"

"I know. I can smell it, too," replied Jerry. "Hell, maybe he brought girls in from Vegas."

"Get serious," I said. "This can't be; Doyle must've washed his hair."

"With *our* water!?" yipped Jerry, with a bigger-than-life voice.

"Ha! Yeah, yeah, Doyle, what's going on?"

We blinked our flashlights into the distant darkness. Again, Doyle's light responded.

"We're still in line, but we better get in quick, the man's lost it!" I stumbled into a rock. "Damn!"

"Maybe a portable shower," said Jerry.

"That my man, we could use."

"Or maybe we just smell so bad that the weeds are taking on a perfume-like aroma," continued Jerry.

"You may be right, but I never smelled weeds like that," and I directed my light toward the ground to get my bearings.

"Pink sage?" quipped Jerry.

"That's not sage," I said matter-of-factly. "That's women!"

We shut up and headed for Doyle's light.

And finally, lo and behold, within earshot, we heard voices. "I'll be damned," Jerry muttered.

"I'll be damned," I agreed, as we stumbled into the blaze of Doyle's gleaming light.

Everything seemed to happen all at once, as we tried to shield our eyes from the blinding brightness. Other lights began to mysteriously dart about as well. They were flashlight beams from other people!

Then there were shouts and hoots. "There they are, there they are!"

Before we understood what was happening, Jerry and I were within a group of people.

Doyle, of course, was there, and so was Brian Bergeson, whom we hadn't seen since Badwater, and at the crossing coming in from Nightmare Canyon.

And yes, *there were women*! Two of them!

They were reporters for a newspaper located in Ridgecrest, California—*The Daily Independent*.

Without hesitation—and to our total surprise and delight—Jerry and I were suddenly bestowed with welcome hugs from the two "angels" who appeared out of nowhere. For one brief, crazy moment, my imagination went into high gear.

There was the overpowering scent of lotions and perfume, of clean, white-scrubbed flesh, soft but firm, and glimpses of blond hair and pink faces along with strobe flashes from cameras that exploded at the same time, bursting into spears of yellow, red, pink, and blue. The wild colors slashed the night, enhancing the aroma of those "fresh-cut flowers."

Anna Pringle and Linda Sappington had picked up a wire story about Jerry and me going across the desert. They struck out, on their own, in hopes of sighting us somewhere along the way—no easy feat. By sheer luck, while driving through the tiny burg of Keeler, located on the eastern edge of the Owens Lake Bed, the two ladies spied a red sports car parked in town. If you knew Keeler, you'd know that a red sports car parked in such a place was an oddity.

Anyway, it was Brian's sports car, and he was sitting in the front seat studying a road map when the two women approached him. They surmised he might have some information about us.

What a surprise to all of them when they discovered they were all looking for the same thing: Doyle and a checkpoint! If they could find Doyle, they'd find Jerry and me.

And they did.

And we met in the night.

Our meeting was short-lived, as everyone had to reluctantly move on, including Jerry and I. We still had to make camp somewhere out there in the dark.

The biggest regret of all, though, was that the women had brought along fresh grapes—just in case they found us.

Jerry and I couldn't take their grapes!

Can you believe that? We couldn't take the grapes!

The trek had to be pure. They could watch and even walk along with us if they so desired, but we couldn't take any offers of additional support, except for water.

The night spread deep and lonely. A cold wind added to the bleak silence as Jerry and I, with flashlights clinched between our teeth, moved rocks around in order to make sleeping bag holes, holes in the dirt, like animals seeking warmth, maybe like men digging for water, whatever.

As I lay in my bag and pulled up the hood close around my head, I realized I was hungry. I was tired.

The wind whistling its solemn lullaby of ancient mystery was a comfort; it had brought us the scent of flowers, the aroma of fresh hair and clean bodies. It reminded us of a better way of life, one that we'd eventually return to.

I saw fleeting glances of blond hair, fresh pink faces, and wild colors slashing at the night.

Suddenly there appeared a giant silver platter with etched handles and engravings. It seemed to be frosted with a light mist; there were packets of C rations, K rations, chocolate cake, fried chicken, and grapes! Misty green grapes! They smelled like fresh-cut flowers.

"Jerry, Jerry! You awake?"

"Go back to sleep," he snorted from a muffled distance.

I did.

CHAPTER 8

DAY 8

Saline Valley

There was the sound of wind swishing about, and for several seconds I had difficulty determining where I was. Instinctively, it felt like morning, an unsettled and restless one, since the veil of darkness had failed to extricate itself.

Finally, I realized I was in my sleeping bag with the hood pulled up over my head. Truly amazing, considering the fact that just a week prior, we weren't even in our bags, let alone inside them with the hoods pulled up tight.

One eye finally opened, the other struggled. Within seconds, the lazy one opened too, mimicking the other.

I located the bag's zipper and pulled it down, in jerks, until—as could be expected—it jammed! I crammed up the other hand to undo it, muttering curses at the small, metal pull tab while I did so. I was able to muster up enough energy to pull it free, and thus, woke myself up. Actually, I didn't want to work that hard so early in what would be another long, drawn-out day.

Whippp! My hood snapped back suddenly as a more than brisk wind was intent on making the morning just a little unpredictable. The hood whipped again, sporadically, and the gust of wind flicked sand into my face. It literally dawned on me that a fine layer of silt lay undetected inside my sleeping bag hood. It had accumulated there throughout the night.

I popped my head clear of the hood and rolled to the downward side of the bag and spat, "...okay wind, you've made your point!"

But something else was different. Besides the wind, the sky was overcast as if a giant screen had been pulled over the entire desert, or perhaps God had tossed sand into the eyes of Mr. Sun, and Mr. Sun was having a hard time seeing Mother Earth. Or maybe it was the other way around. Jerry and I were the ones out of focus, out of sync.

We had wished for an easier send-off, and we had it on that morning. The trade off? Cold versus heat, silence versus wind, dark versus light.

Jerry's bag—with him in it—was about thirty feet to my right and upwind. His sleeping bag hood was also flapping and making a whipped, flag-like noise. Besides my own bag making crazy noises, I realized I'd been hearing his also, all through the night. All the while, I thought I'd been hearing—dreaming perhaps?—of skirts blowing in the wind with an occasional effervescent whiff of fresh-cut flowers. With the wind the way it was, and the frame of mind I was in, that suggestion was entirely plausible.

We greeted the new day, and the drab, colder-than-usual atmosphere was bound to set the stage for the two of us, as if earth itself somehow was to be our precipitator. It would set our mood, or so it seemed. In reality, the indignities of the dawning were actually quite pleasant. With heat, you sweat; you're uncomfortable as tiny beads of moisture run amuck across your body. Your mind warns you that this is only the front end of the day, and as the sun would arch higher, it would only become more intolerable.

A cold morning turns the opposite: you liven to the snap, knowing full well that it's bound to get warmer as the day stretches toward the same eventual horizon.

With storms, well, that's another matter. If you awaken to the wet, it can be miserable from square one. If it's just overcast and threatening, maybe there's a chance of packing up and moving out before it actually strikes. If you've had a chance to pack early and most of your gear is drawn up tight, you shouldn't get everything wet. Only you—on the outside.

Traveling in a storm? You get wet and tired. Stop, tent up? More cold, more wet? Take your pick.

It wasn't that kind of a choice on that eighth morning. We'd simply pack up, move out, and be thankful for the cool overcast. It didn't feel like rain, only a change in the weather. Winter wasn't too far off.

But the comfort of the morning was a hoax, and we knew it. Sure, nice and easy at our 5,000 foot elevation. That wasn't a problem at all. But what about twelve or thirteen or fourteen thousand feet? That *would* be a problem! In our own silence, we pondered that.

Yes, winter was on the way. It would eventually roll in like a monstrous freight train in the night. We'd hear the lonely whistle and the harsh, metallic sounds—the wind and the thunder—in the black darkness. We'd run to make it to the crossing before the gate would close us out, and the thing that would be so unnerving would be the fact that men can be foolhardy enough to risk crossing the gate at the last moment. It would be an all-or-none decision, we'd think about that in the days ahead.

We were just a ways off the Saline Valley Road. Within a mile, we crossed over and headed northwest, holding to our 280 degree compass course that put us dead-on for the Santa Rosa Mine. Doyle would find it easy enough as the road would eventually cut off in that direction. No big deal. Just find the road, and head right for the mine.

Doyle did just that. So did Jerry and I, with the exception of coming in much later.

The wind and overcast subsided and disappeared, respectively, by the time we reached the site. A warm, midday sun was, for once, a welcome entity. It was no longer a harsh, relentless heat that threatened our very existence but a soothing warmth that encouraged our efforts. It made us feel like working, a far cry from the dread monotony and worry for the lack of water and the dangers of hiking midday.

Sure, we still had to have water, but it wasn't on the same order of priority as it had been a few days before.

The Santa Rosa Mine itself was even a welcome addition. It would've made a great shelter during extreme heat—or cold. In our case, we'd just explore and then move on. Had it been nightfall, however, or a storm, we would've made good use of the location.

I flashed back to the many episodes of past desert travel, the days of solo work going from mine shaft to mine shaft and tunnel to tunnel during stormy and cold weather. I'd sleep near the openings, never knowing what was deep inside the shaft, behind or below me. Nor did I want to know. I'm not keen on cave exploration, especially by myself.

The Santa Rosa was no exception. The three of us—Jerry, Doyle, and I—went deep inside the cavern with flashlights. It was massive!

Water hoses and air pipes led far into the depths with a grand finale open space that housed a huge tank, or boiler, or whatever. It was at that point that I'd had enough of the underground. On our way out, we discovered a dead dog: a *mummified* dead dog!

He lay as still as stone. His well-preserved, dirt-blond fur coat was a grim reminder that things, and beings, do expire in such a land devoid of water, but they do so with grace and dignity. It's similar to those unfortunates who've frozen to death where the water source is at the other extreme. All this, as opposed to the traumatic deaths of war, or the jungle, where beings are either torn apart or rot into putrefaction because of a humid atmosphere.

This dog had—surely, not by choice—expired in a land so dry and parched that decomposition was held at bay until such time that bone and muscle finally crumbles and withers away. How long does it take? How old was the dog? How'd he—or she—get there in the first place? Was it starvation? Thirst? Was there suffering?

We could relate to that. Would there be suffering for Jerry and I without water?

Good man, Doyle.

Please be there, just be there with the water!

And Doyle *was* there with the water.

Even though the Santa Rosa was an easy checkpoint, and we'd just seen Doyle the night before, there would be no allowance for complacency, and there was a strange emptiness as we watched Doyle drive away and Jerry and I prepared ourselves to move on to the next point.

We'd not see Doyle again for awhile, and the two of us would treasure our two quarts of water, each.

Our midday meal was meager since we'd begun rationing our food supply to one-half the normal. We had to hold off, at least until Lone Pine. In fact, that would be the rule, period! Lone Pine was the only chance for resupply, and it was two, maybe three days, distant.

We hiked our way over the top of the Santa Rosa Mine, heading west, in a direction toward the Inyo crest. We were already on the lower, east slope of that range, the crest lay along the horizon.

We no longer had to squint or use Jerry's binos to pick out, on occasion, the mighty Sierra, the next range over. The Mighty One was there all right, due west, towering and forbidden-looking, beckoning those of us who look from the east.

One has to appreciate the early-day travelers, heading west, believing that their travel direction would get them to the ocean, the Sierras being the last obstacle—but not quite!

The Malpais Plateau, the Inyo Range, and the Owens Valley were yet to be crossed, with a ton of desert in between. Then there would be the Alabamas, then another dry stretch, then the climb to the Whitney Crest, and, for us, the top of Mt. Whitney, the Mother, the Granddaddy, the alpha of our own journey!

We continued west, easing ourselves up and across the Inyos. The pitch became so steep that it required dug-in boot toes and grabbed-on hands: a spider crawl might have been the best term to describe it as we worked our way, diagonally, across the lower deep-sand canyons. We would lip one, only to discover the same conditions on the next two rises, then the next three, four, and beyond.

The final climb netted us a broad-reaching mesa that strangely resembled the spine of an ancient creature. Joshuas dotted the landscape like erratic dorsal fins. Suddenly, the name Malpais began to manifest itself. It was the *Bad Land:* sterile, crooked, sandpaper-like. I hefted my pack just so I could hear my water bottles slosh; I thought of our scant lunch and worried about the next supper and how we'd split the noodles. I thought about the mummified dog in the mine, I hoped we'd see Doyle again soon, somewhere up ahead, in a night or so.

The sun was setting against a streamer-like sky: streaks of soft drift stretched, north to south, across the distant western peaks as if runs of drab paint had somehow been spilled onto a slow moving conveyer belt.

Those clouds were on the move, moving toward us at a fast clip. And then the wind began, and then we understood the movement of the clouds. The blowing gusts had finally caught up to us after lying dormant since morning.

The further we went, the windier it got and the flatter and more bizarre the land became.

The Joshuas became our Easter Island statues. How had those strange trees come about? Maybe they *were* statues, but those things, supposedly, were alive. But is that so with statues and headstones? What about rocks and earth?

We continued on and the sun bowed out as if it didn't want to stay around for the finale. Mr. Sun had watched us struggle too many times and had probably seen enough. El Sol could simply write us off, close the door, and let us be.

We, too, watched the struggles of life from our own peculiar perspective. When we've seen enough, we simply turn the switch.

The wind continued in earnest. It roared in from the west, and the mist that seemed to enshroud us so mysteriously, in reality, was silt dust blowing up from the Owens Dry Lake Bed. It wasn't desert wind, per se, but a cold, mountain wind dropping down off the Sierras, raging across the open lake bed, and then smashing, headlong, into the Inyos.

As it became darker, we began to scan the landscape for any kind of shelter: rock, bluff, anything. Even a gully or an arroyo would give us a bit of relief from a wind that was becoming increasingly colder.

Even without additional protection, we'd still be using our tent. However, it's still standard practice to get the best you can in way of earthly protection, tent or no tent.

Without wasting the remaining light of day, we settled into the first depression we came to, our home away from home, a rock-strewn gutter with a solitary bush to our westerly side. It would do just fine.

An hour later, we lay huddled in the small, but quite adequate, two-man tent. Jerry held his flashlight beam on my hands as I tried to repair my own light. I had dropped it onto a rock while trying to peg the backside of the tent into the crusty soil. Jerry yelled something from up front, trying to be heard above the roar of the wind and the flapping and dashing of the tent. All hands were at work—literally—as the wind tried its best to insult us with its airborne antics that would come and go with blast force.

With flashlight in mouth, I answered back, forgetting where my flashlight was. Well, you guessed it: *Bergthold, you dumb, stupid shit*!

I puttered with a small piece of twist-em wire and tweezers as Jerry's own light would dim bright to low. To keep his own flashlight from going sour, he'd bang the damn thing against the side of his boot, and we'd continue on with the operation.

The wind would cause the tent to flap and heave, and we'd curse a little, while at the same time, praising the little tent for doing such a good job.

"There. That'll do!" I proclaimed, as my light came back to life. "Just like new," and we both kind of chuckled. It was time to eat.

"Back on schedule," said Jerry as he folded the empty noodle package. We both had licked our separate halves clean.

Jerry mimicked smacking his lips. "Mighty good, real good."

"Just as fine as wine in the summertime," I quipped, while at the same time feeling for my water bottles at my side.

We'd had a heck of a time heating water for our noodles. We had hunkered down on the leeward side of the tent trying to settle the wind that battered our stove. It blew out twice, but we persisted and, finally, produced warm water with half-cooked noodles. We topped off supper with dried apricots and cocoa. Then we crawled into the tent to work on my light and to get out of the wind that almost felt like it might be dying down.

"Your bottles inside?" I asked. "Probably freeze tonight if that wind quits."

There was a brief silence. Jerry cocked his head: "Listen!" he said, softly. "The wind *is* trying to die."

We both listened.

"Yeah, yeah," I whispered, hoarsely.

Jerry stretched, working his water bottles into sort of a pillow. I lay back, in the opposite direction, trying to smooth out my sleeping bag.

"Yeah, it's gonna quit; it'll freeze, sure as hell."

Jerry chuckled, "Sure as hell," as he wadded up his slouch hat, still trying to make a pillow out of his bottles.

I drifted off. "Mighty fine noodles, mighty fine."

And the wind was settling down.

CHAPTER 9

DAY 9

Malpais Plateau

Jerry and I awoke early, both at the same time. We were almost to the point of being excited and anxious because we knew, from the night before, that we'd awaken to a different kind of morning. We were right! There was a cold, snappy feel to the air; it was fresh and zesty.

My head was next to the zipped-up tent opening, and I turned and slapped at the door flap with the back of my hand. There was a spattering sound and then a swish. The sounds were not unfamiliar. It was ice and frost! I had splintered the crusty ice seal that evidently covered the entire tent, and the frozen stuff slid off the front. It was like snow sliding off a roof.

"Good gawd!" I yelped, as I stuck my head through the unzipped door flap. "It's like winter out here!" I crawled out of the tent.

Jerry was right behind me and, for a brief moment, as I glanced back, he looked like jolly St. Nick coming down—or through—a chimney. I expected sleigh bells.

"Whoaaa!" he chimed. "It's Christmas time!"

How appropriate.

Standing upright, we surveyed the white land. We were struck by the most unusual sight: a white, tingly layer of frost everywhere and on everything: our poncho-covered packs, the tent, the rocks, the earth, and the bush next to the tent that now looked like a flocked Christmas tree.

Our breaths, when talking to one another, and ourselves, produced tiny puffs of misty clouds; our urine produced steam!

The surrounding Joshua trees were stoic in their pristine, wind-bent positions, and the scraggly trunks and branches suddenly made me aware of myself, and Jerry, and how we must look to others, if only others were about.

The St. Nick image of Jerry dissipated as quickly as our steaming did. Jerry was gaunt—not jolly gaunt, but tough gaunt! I felt for my own ribs and could feel them easily.

My hip bones were evident, and I watched Jerry as he walked away. He wasn't the same man, neither was I.

We were tough and sinewy, and I continued watching Jerry as he moved with precision and how he swung his steps, not staggeringly so, but striking and moving with sure footing. Yes, the point man!

I would not dare imagine ourselves as tired and beat. I—we—couldn't believe in that; a negative reaction would only result in negative results. There has to be a positive will to succeed, the will to continue.

The Joshuas were tough, and they'd been there for as long as we wished them to be. They didn't whine or bend but stood solid and took it all in stride: the winds, the storms, the heat, and the cold. In this white of morning, it was as if they were reaching out and saying, "come, follow, be strong!" I felt renewed.

The thrill of it all was manifested by a brilliant sunshine that poked over the eastern ridge, low-lighting all the ice and the frost. It was truly a sight to behold.

I skittered along the depression where we'd pegged down our tent the night before and then cut northward, to the next slope. I turned my back to the sun, when suddenly, something shadowed me.

I swung around. I was astounded!

Fog was roiling up all around our small encampment. It seemed to have come from outer space, and I stood in awe and just stared at the heavy mist as it engulfed everything.

Not that I'd never seen fog—I knew it well. I'd seen deep, thick tule fog from the San Joaquin Valley, but this was unique. The Joshuas, high desert plateau, and fog!

Everything was suddenly transformed into a wondrous dreamland, and Jerry and I yelled back and forth, excitedly, like tiny tugboats, lost in the night, trying to get true bearings.

We continued our walkabout, exploring our newfound world of mist and clouds. Within an hour, however, the fog lifted, and Mr. Sun looked back in on us as if nothing was out of the ordinary.

The earth reheated, quickly, forcing us to shed our cold-weather clothing, one piece at a time, until we were back to square one: me, in shorts and Jerry with shirt, trousers, and his old slouch hat.

By the time we had everything dried and packed—and pieces of ice and frost shoved into our water bottles—it was business as usual: warm, desert, and heading west.

It was probably around two in the afternoon by the time we finally worked our way across the highest point of the huge mesa called Malpais. And it was at that juncture—the western edge—that we finally began to understand what the connotation of Malpais, or Bad Land, was really all about.

We literally found ourselves standing along the edge of a 7,000 foot overlook.

My heart raced as we came to the edge.

Right before us, right in front of us, the earth eroded away to the bone-bleached chutes below.

And what a stretch it was all coming to be: to be so elated with such a magnificent early morning, to stand and view the Sierras from such a viewpoint, to feel like a bird, to be so free, and to feel the blood rush with excitement, to experience the warrior-like strength.

Again, before us, with a distance of probably ten to fifteen miles, lay the vast, ever-encompassing Owens Valley. The wind was heading our way, again, and we knew this by the swirls of distant dust patterns over the valley. It would be only a matter of time before those renewed winds would be upon us, like the day before.

Beyond the Owens Valley—and the huge, valley-shaped dry lake bed—was the Sierra Nevada. How many times had Jerry and I looked up to those mountains from the highway or from the Alabamas, but never from where we then stood.

But those cliffs! North, south, as far as we could see, and we were smack-dab in the middle!

It was impact! We both felt it! We'd really hit the wall.

The hell you say! What wall?

We walked in small, nervous circles. *What would we do? Jump? No, asshole! No, no, no!*

Our imaginations were jumping track, but we really didn't have to talk about it at all. We had to think, work it out.

We knew we'd get out, but with the delays and the time involved, that place wasn't about to turn us loose.

But that's the way it goes. We'd simply have to work it out. Were those cliffs really that much of a setback, an obstacle? No, not really.

The fact of the matter is, *Ahh, I've got it! Denial! Yes, that's it. The cliff is just the tip of the barn, so they say.*

No, no, no! It's not really the cliff, it's the Sierras, damn it, dead ahead! We could see clouds building to the north, and it was October; winter was coming, and we were trying to get to 13,000 and 14,000 feet!

We're idiots! We're stupid! We're nuts!

And we were alone, our own thoughts. Control, that's it. Don't lose it. Be cool. Think!

"Okay, Jerry," I said, sternly, after each of us had walked each flank: "Whaddaya got?"

"Pull south," he replied, with confidence. "Catch it down the line."

"Only way," I said. "I've nothing over here; it gets worse," and I cocked my head toward the north.

We stood together with sunburned eyes, squinting and tearing. We looked toward the direction of an advancing wind, pointing south, tracing it out, talking, and planning.

Visually, I followed Jerry's point-finger.

"We've got to follow that hog-back," I mumbled. "See, it cuts down."

"Yeah," he said. "Then it disappears, but I'll bet it picks up, lower down, hell-of-a lot a scree, volcanic."

"You got it," I replied. "Slip-and-slide-with-Sam-and-Clyde."

"It'll pull us off a bit from our 280, but we got no choice."

"Just another damn detour. Hang in there, Doyle, we're on the way," and my soliloquy drifted with the growing wind.

Our plan wasn't that far off. We simply could not follow, straight-on, over such a drop-off. It was like Zabriskie Point, only ten times worse.

So, we'd cut south, roughly a mile, and then follow a serpentine spine down to a lower elevation. At that point, we'd have to reevaluate.

And, as is always the case—mountain and desert—it looks like one thing from one point, but you can bet on it being totally different once you get there.

We'd gamble that we'd be able to continue on from the new point.

We checked our water bottles as they thawed, we were pleased at our new-found water supply of ice and frost. We'd scraped all we could from our tent and ponchos, earlier, and squished the handfuls into our bottles. We had a good quart apiece, even after supper from the night before and not seeing Doyle for some twenty-four hours.

Then again, we had a long haul ahead of us, and there'd be no telling how long it would take us to get off the mesa and down into Keeler—or at least to the outskirts—hopefully, to a tiny, nondescript, boot hill-type of cemetery, at the edge of that small community.

That's where Doyle would be waiting.

Jerry and I were still grappling with a hit-the-wall breakdown. We were both well aware of the overload phenomenon of pushing hard for seven and eight days, knowing full well that we'd eventually have to have considerable rest. The deprivations had been too great, too heavy. We were literally up against an emotional wall. It's always at such a point in time that men—and women—can crumble. Looks and stature have no bearing, it's all mental; it's what's inside that counts when the chips are down, and the price of poker suddenly goes up.

We continued to lull around, and walked without our packs in opposite directions. We had to have self-talk, self-think; we had to cry to ourselves, whine, and conjure up our own self-pity. We had to start thinking of home and of showers, women, and food: fried chicken and chocolate cake. We had to take advantage of the privilege of hating the ground: the dirt, the sand, the wind, the rocks, the cliffs, the scree, the talus, and serpentine ridges.

The caveman life is tough; nobody gets the promised Rose Garden, the milk and honey.

How'd the miners do it, the pioneers?

Shit! We've got it lucky. We've got Doyle driving around in a mechanical box that goes anywhere and everywhere. All you have to do is put a chemical in a tank and away you go.

At home, we had everything we could possibly want. How can there be poor people? Destitution? *People starving in America? With a TV antenna on the house and a Cadillac® out front. Those people are poor?*

Bullshit! Go to China, India, Africa, Death Valley, Malpais Plateau.

Jerry and I came together. We clasped hands, briefly, and stared hard into each others faces.

"Yo, partner, let's kick ass!"

We cut south, to a point that led due west. It was a slick-topped, gravel-strewn ridge that formed an angle that resembled a tented rooftop, one steep slope meeting another in typical ridge-back fashion.

The coloring of the earthen scree was volcanic, covering the gamut from serpentine green-yellow to dirty tan, to purple and black. And the darker colors drew a renewed strength from the sun, which to us, meant heat!

Once again, the penetrating desert environment was upon and all around us. By midday, thermal pressure finally produced the expected rise in temperature as the sun slid past high noon. Maybe it was all due to the fact that the wind, that tried its best earlier, suddenly became almost nonexistent.

Visually, we studied the landscape. We eyeballed the long, slender, precarious stretch of ridge as if searching for something we'd lost the day before. *We had lost something! Patience!*

Day in and day out had been a puzzle, a challenge. For just once, we would've reveled in declaring a clear and undisputable route. A route that would get us through for sure, one that wouldn't necessitate the total reliance on water or us being concerned by the threat of being cornered or trapped on some teetering ledge or ridgeline that we couldn't back out of, or go forward from.

Of course, if this all were to have been a cakewalk, we would've searched for just the opposite.

Man is strange in that regard. Take away the challenge, the threat, the danger, and I'll be damned if he doesn't absolutely go the other way until he finds just that! The challenge!

And by "patience," I simply imply, "eagerness!" We could see where we wanted to go—to be—but getting there would always be another matter.

The thought of giving up is not what I speak of. In fact, to have even considered such a notion would, in our determined estimation, be synonymous with the lack of self-esteem; at worst, it would be cowardly. Men, especially, will always be faced with this concept, at one time or another during a lifetime, and the many shapes and forms of this 'rite of passage' will manifest itself in the strangest of ways. For Jerry and me, it would be the ability to conquer a part of the natural world's unknown. Perhaps, it would be the solo experience, to pit oneself against the dark, the forbidden, the unknown, but doing so on your own terms, by your lonesome.

This has nothing to do with physical strength, per se, but what's going on inside one's mind. After all, it's our own evolved limbic systems that can become our greatest enemy. We have feelings and emotions, and they leave us vulnerable.

In the long run, we fear ourselves; we fear for the ones we'd leave behind, when, in reality, we'd feel nothing, personally. No, we'd be free, and the ones left behind would then become the fearful ones, and the cycle would continue.

We could see where the ridge terminated, but that was all. Subconsciously, we were computing an escape route. Could we return the same way if it didn't work out at the end?

Following a spine is always tricky, because it eventually ends with a severe drop-off and then you have to find a way down. If you follow the trenches, they also end, and then you have to find a way up! And that's what's so frustrating; that's when patience goes to the wind, so to speak.

Yes, we could see the valley below, but getting there would take some figuring out.

Right off the bat, the ridge turned bad! It was so slick with scree that for probably the first thirty yards, we worked hand to foot; hand-gripping the ridge bone itself where possible, and then, and only then, would foot placement follow. It was the old spider crawl once again. It was slow and laborious, and then the ridge came to an end! And yes, it dropped off, severely!

We roped around the top ledge, or rather, around a bald-faced piece of granite—or 'black rock.' We did so reluctantly, we really had to make sure that that topper would hold. As it was—and as had been the case all through the desert—there would be pieces of hard rock jutting up from a soil-cement base. Most of the time, you'd have to literally pick and chop to break the rascals free. But on just as many other occasions, those rocks would simply pop loose and you'd be hanging in mid-air with rock-in-hand—but separated from the planet—big time!

We pulled and tugged on the rope hoping it would hold.

"Okay, who's first?"

"Me!"

"No, me!"

"Don't be a dumb-shit, I'll go."

"No, I'll drop my pack, pass it down, I'll go."

"No! You got family."

"Well, what do you call your kids?"

"Bullshit! I go!"

"Me"

"No, me!"

We began to laugh. Our relief finally came through; we could always count on the break, a fresh way of looking through a tense situation. We both knew that if the rope didn't hold, we could wind up in one hell of a situation—at the bottom of a non-climbable pit!

But at that moment, we couldn't have cared less.

"You're really gonna look stupid down there without a casket!"

"Ha! Burial above ground. Say, did I ever tell you a..."

And we'd laugh at our corny jokes and jibes.

"Just let my cat know, he's got a copy of my will."

"Who's your attorney? This is a big break for your wife."

"My kids will say, 'He's where? Is he with a woman? He musta burned-up his donkey brake!'"

"Bureau of Land Management is gonna raise hell with us for littering up one of their canyons; my frying pan, no doubt, will go to the Smithsonian."

And on and on.

There we were, perched on a file-like precipice with a thin thread of rope looped over a chunk of rock that might or *might not* hold in a world so remote from imagination that words would never be able to describe or explain.

I couldn't even begin to mess with my camera as both hands were totally involved with the task of keeping everything else together. Nor would it record accurately what I—we—were really seeing, feeling, or doing.

We were mere specks of sand in a giant pile of doo-doo, in a wild place where we'd probably never be found if something really failed or didn't work.

Yet, we could see the sublime, the ridiculous, the humor.

"So, we go the bottom, big friggin' deal," said Jerry, with reservation. "Put me on your shoulders."

"Yeah, right, one hundred feet down."

We flipped a tiny rock to see who'd go first. It rolled and fell over the side.

I volunteered.

I slipped out of my pack. Now Jerry really had his hands full. He had to handle the rope and care for his own pack and mine. He ran an arm through one of my straps.

I took both strands of rope, and, facing the wall, toed and slid my way to the bottom. All the way down I moaned, "I don't like this, I don't like this."

I reached the bottom. "Hold on, let me check," I said and scurried over to the next rise and looked over. "Okay! We got it. We can go on to the next."

Then came my pack, sliding, skidding, and bouncing, all the while knocking away loose sand and tiny pieces of gravel. I spat and turned my face away to protect my eyes, I was ready to catch my pack if it would've broken loose.

Next came Jerry's pack, the same way, then Jerry.

"You the last one?" I quipped as he was halfway down the chute, I knew he was in full concentration on what he was doing. He stopped to think about what I'd just asked; it came through on delay. He laughed.

Jerry would not have come down until we knew for sure it was clear up ahead. This would be our tactic time and time again: one would scout ahead until a new route was picked, the rear man holding tight just in case we had to back out.

At the next chute, we reversed positions. Jerry went ahead. It was tougher than the first because we had to work around a rock-point that jutted, outwardly, halfway down. It broke off in Jerry's lap—literally!

"Hey, how's it taste down there?" Jerry was spitting and trying to get the crap out of his face.

"It's loose!" he yelled up, finally.

"No shit!" I yelled back.

What a deduction, what a profundity! Our mental acuity was definitely astounding.

By late afternoon, we were sitting next to a blowing-wind sand dune, at a three-quarter-way-down location. We'd pulled off the worst of the Inyo Range. We were admiring an old turn-of-the-century canteen that I inadvertently stubbed my toe on in what we would refer to as Canteen Canyon, our last deep-sand trench, off of Inyo, which put us almost onto the desert floor proper.

As the afternoon headed toward the downside of another day, the wind, once again, became stronger and stronger.

And as the rigors of the day slowly crept into our physical beings, exhaustion was slowly bringing us to a humble ending.

We laid with our backs toward the blowing wind; taking down the last of our water, knowing—hoping—we'd be meeting up with Doyle sometime during the night.

The wind gusts grew stronger and more erratic; we'd pulled on our night clothes, which included wind hoods pulled up tight around our heads and necks to keep out the blowing pieces of sand and grit. We took turns, spitting, downwind, and our voices were becoming hoarse.

Suddenly, all around us, the dunes, the sky, and all the earth began to turn colors. Sun streaks broke through the mighty clouds that finally made it down from the north, now to our west, enshrouding the western flank of the Owens Valley and the eastern flank of the Sierras.

The sand dunes we'd suddenly encountered presented a mysterious sidelight into what finally looked like true desert. We'd been over millions of tons of rock and eroded soil, parched and sandpapered, but this was the first *real sand*!

And in that setting sun, we felt an impact that was a cross between strength and emotional lassitude. In short, we were worn, but elated. That desert country hadn't put us down yet.

Hungry, tired, ragged, and thirsty, we two old men would yet see the Owens Valley. We'd get water from Doyle that night, and maybe see Lone Pine by tomorrow night.

"Hope so, hope so!"

Damn! We were hungry!

It was close to ten o'clock, after nightfall, and we were roughly a mile or so above Highway 136/190, when we first saw the car's headlights.

"There's the road," I said, excitedly. "Dead on!"

"How sweet it is," exclaimed Jerry. "We're getting there, that's the road that'll go right past Keeler and the cemetery."

It was Highway 136/190 and it stretched, north to south, from Keeler to Darwin, or, in a broader context, from Lone Pine to Death Valley. We'd be intersecting with that same road as we worked our way, downward, from our southeast position. We knew exactly where we were and the direction we had to go in order to reach the cemetery. We were coming in at an angle, like the cutting of a giant pie, the apex being a set of lights, which were barely visible to our north.

"That has to be Keeler," said Jerry, continuing, as we moved in closer together. "Those far lights might be Swansea, don't know for sure."

"There's nobody at Swansea, is there?" I asked. "Isn't that just an old abandoned site?"

"Could be," and Jerry banged his flashlight against his leg as the tiny light beam, flickered. "Damn light, not much better than yours."

I banged mine against the palm of my opposite hand. It, too, was going dim, but it was functional.

Our flashlights just barely lit up the rugged ground that was strewn with rocks and brush. It was rough, real rough, especially in the dark, with a headwind that seemed to make everything move, made things noisy. After a while, it would make one nervous and tense, like animals who become super alert when the wind blows hard.

Because of the boisterous wind and all the rustling sounds around us, we couldn't hear the occasional car that would zip by below. This forced us to operate on visual alone, concentrating on the lights ahead. *Were we actually seeing the light of Keeler? Are there lights, at all, at Swansea? What about Doyle's light?*

The cemetery should've been south of Keeler, proper, but maybe it's situated so close to Keeler that from our low-angled view-point, Doyle's light might appear to be intermingled with the others that dotted the night.

As we drew closer, we were hopeful that his light would begin to separate from the few others. We also knew that there shouldn't be any other lights at the cemetery, only Doyle's.

Finally—and it seemed like forever—our orientation became clearer. The highway was definitely to our left and

Keeler was dead ahead. We started picking up a blinking light from where the cemetery should've been.

"I think he's got us," I said, moving in closer to Jerry so we could hear one another over the wind. "See? Isn't he blinking?"

"Yeah, yeah," said Jerry, straining to see. "Yeah, that's him. Its Doyle, he's flashing on and off. Look! Just to the right."

We both stopped and strained to see. Even without using Jerry's binos, we could pick out a tiny light, now separated from other distant ones, blinking on and off. It had to be Doyle.

Within the next hour, thrashing through the brush at an even faster pace, we walked into the brilliant glare of Doyle's now bigger-than-life spotlight!

His truck was parked so that the front end was facing into the wind; his spotlight was hoisted up, above, and attached to a metal alloy pole that swayed back-and-forth with the impatient wind.

Doyle had water ready for us as we literally stumbled into the glare of his mighty light. The fumbling around was not the result of fatigue, but rather from the intense brightness of the makeshift searchlight put together by the water man.

And as you can imagine, it all made for some very interesting comments from Jerry and me, but of course, the light was friendly and we wouldn't have had it any other way. We heaped praise on Doyle as we high-fived greetings all the way around.

Without hesitation, Doyle was anxious to give us the latest weather report. It wasn't good; the first big storm of the season was rolling down from the north.

We fought with the tent getting it up in the wind; we had sand, in and with our dinner. Doyle was sure there were ghosts in the cemetery, and Jerry and I were preparing to sleep amongst them.

Too tired to discuss, in detail, all the monumental problems of the day, we all said screw it, and headed for our sleeping bags. Jerry and I went to the tent, and Doyle to his truck. We slept, solid, until the light of the next windy morning.

CHAPTER 10

DAY 10

Keeler Cemetery

"October 23, 1989: wind still blowing but not as cold as it was up on the 7,000-ft. plateau...sun not up yet...heavy clouds overhead may hold it back...more clouds hanging low, the west...."

I closed my journal and crawled outside. It was the first time that Doyle had camped at our checkpoint location. Even so, he held to himself; he slept in his truck, ate his own food, and drank his own coffee—Jerry and I weren't coffee drinkers anyway. In general, he was the water man, and that was it.

Doyle was already up when Jerry and I crawled out of the tent.

"Morning, Doyle," I said.

Doyle just stood for a moment, and stared. "You guys look like hell!"

Believe it or not, it was great to hear him say so. He was not only the water man, he was also the witness to what others might not believe; that we really had come this far, that we really were at the Keeler cemetery, and that we *really did* look like hell!

Doyle, in turn, was a welcome sight. He looked great!

"What are you comparing us to?" I asked, as I pulled my sleeping bag and pad out of the tent.

"Well," and he thought about it briefly, "you look as good as that rock over there," and he half-assed pointed.

"You mean that wrinkly thing?" We chuckled as the three of us milled around the leeward side of Doyle's truck to get out of the wind, our jacket hoods already flapping like wind socks.

Doyle kept on. "Next time you guys oughta try hiking in country that has lakes and streams and such."

"What the hell you talking about?" Jerry chimed in. "There's lakes all around us. Dry maybe, but they're lakes!"

We laughed.

It was a relief to have Doyle around. He—and his truck—provided a brief respite from the tedium of the day-to-day isolation. But there was other relief as well, we could see signs of life around us.

The Keeler cemetery was right off the highway, telephone poles ran alongside, parallel. In the near distance, we could see the outbuildings of Keeler, and if you weren't used to seeing *anything* at all in way of civilization, then Keeler would be a welcome sight. If you'd just driven in from the city, Keeler would still be a sight, but from a totally different perspective.

"Sure looks and feels like storm," said Jerry, glumly, looking up to a sky that was having a tough time making up its mind as to what it might do.

"Well," said Doyle, "can't do much about it, just do what you can. You guys have done great even if you don't get to Whitney."

"If it'd start to squirt right now, I'd be happy that we got this far," I concluded. "But we'll go further, we'll not quit!"

"No, not now!" said Jerry, in earnest. "Besides, it's not that cold down here."

"No, not here, but what about up there?" I gestured toward the west.

"Yes siree. Big Uncle awaits, you betcha," Doyle said as he tossed the last of his coffee to the wind.

I mumbled something about getting to a water hose so we could rinse off, anything.

We proceeded to pack up.

It was music to our ears when, as Doyle drove away, he shouted back to us: "See you in Lone Pine!"

Yes siree. Lone Pine, come-hell-or-high-water, rain or snow, or sunshine.

The wind continued its drive as it thrust down from the distant northeast, which meant we'd have a side-headwind. That was actually in our favor since most of any new dust that might be kicked up, later on, would be moving toward the south. We'd hang tight to the northwest, our only alternative. We'd already accepted the fact that we had roughly twelve to fifteen miles to cross over what would amount to be another ancient sea bottom, or lake bed: the Owens Valley Dry Lake Bed to be exact. Big difference: there was water out in the middle—lots of it! And along the shoreline—similar to the bogs of Death Valley—there would be tons of viscous mud and sponge dirt that would allow one to sink up to their eyeballs, or otherwise, if one wasn't careful.

If we trekked south, we'd have to go twenty miles or so until we'd be able to cross again. By going north, we'd be holding to our original 280 degree course by compass, but again, by going north there'd be a payback. We'd have to eventually cross the Owens River, which flowed north to south, and it was that very river that dumped into the giant lake that lay due west of us.

The early morning low ceiling clouds finally lifted and the sun, once again, dominated. It seemed to make the wind more vicious, however, and we could see fresh dust clouds already forming toward the southern most end of the valley. We were lucky—at least at that point—that the wind was blowing in the direction it was, because the Owens Valley dust is a mean hombre to have to deal with.

It's a silt dust, very fine and cutting—destructive—and of the few residents who do reside in Keeler, most live with oxygen bottles at the ready. If the winds reverse and plow into Keeler from across the dry lake bed—regardless of the water out in the middle—on go the oxygen masks.

Indeed, Owen's Valley dust is a health hazard: Valley Fever, asthma, bronchitis, emphysema, not a good mix.

Fortunately—for Keelerites, anyway—most of the dust blows north to south, and the winds drive the tiny dust particles toward the Antelope Valley, where Jerry and I are from, some one hundred miles or so away. The fine, silica-like dust is even a detriment to jet aircraft that operate out of that west Mojave region. Jet intakes are sensitive, so are men's lungs.

Across the highway and into Keeler we went. It was like moving back in time to the 1800's.

Keeler was actually an old dock town for the then full-of-water Owens Lake. The town developed and was busiest in the late 1800s, supplying the nearby mines of the Cerro Gordo which are situated in the range just east of the town, the same Inyo Range that Jerry and I just humped off of.

Bullion from that mine financed the early development of Los Angeles. Keeler was the southern end of the line for the Carson and Colorado narrow gauge railroad, and as Jerry and I got closer to the heart of town, we could see the depot that still remained. It stood alone, like a ghost.

The few vintage 50's and 60's automobiles that suddenly sprang into view made us recall how Brian Bergeson's little red sports car must've drawn—and did draw—the attention of the two lady reporters who met us in the Saline Valley. The imaginary scent of fresh-cut flowers was again, suddenly, heavy on my mind. The few contemporary mobile homes that also came into view were practically the only reminders that it really was the 1980's.

In ten minutes, we were practically out of town.

But wait!

"Look at that! A post office!"

And there was.

An American flag flapped overhead, and a simple sign underneath: U.S. Post Office, Keeler, California.

We approached.

Opening the front door was like opening the whole wall. It was the size of a 1940's shoe shine stand, a second partition separated us from the door, and there was a middle-aged lady behind the tiny, grilled cubbyhole.

She looked startled, and if she had spoken right then, I would have imagined her saying, "And what mine you-all boys from?"

But she didn't say anything, just stared. Seconds ticked away, but it seemed like minutes.

"Ma'am," I said, as I moved closer to the miniature window, while at the same time adjusting my pack so I wouldn't bump the wall, "are you open for business?" I had to lean over to look into the window, my pack causing me to squat down, just a bit.

"Why yes, yes I am," she replied.

Jerry was still having a hard time closing the front door, and we were bumping into each other.

"We'd like a favor, ma'am," I continued.

"Yes, how can I help?" The lady appeared genuinely surprised at seeing strange men, especially with packs on their backs. In reality, she probably saw the same Keeler faces day in and day out, year after year, but packs?

"Ahhh," I hesitated. "My partner and I, we...we just walked in from Death Valley, and its taken us nine or ten days, and we'd appreciate it if you could take your date stamp; well, could you stamp the date on a piece of paper and then sign it?"

"Well," the lady hesitated.

"We'd like to have you verify that we were actually here."

"Why yes. I can do that." She reached for her stamp and a piece of paper. "Where are you heading for?"

"Whitney!" Jerry said, shuffling in the back.

"Oh, not the top?" she exclaimed with surprise. "Winter's comin' on, it's almost November!"

"The top!" continued Jerry, laconically.

There Must Have Been an Angel

I nodded in the affirmative. "The top!"

"Oh my," and her voice trailed off as she busied herself with the note.

She finished and passed the small piece of paper to me. I glanced at it quickly. It was perfect:

> *"Hope you make it to the top"*
> *Martha Trent, Postmaster*
> *Keeler, CA 93530*
> *October 23, 1989*
> *USPS*

(original date-stamped document on file)

We thanked her, bid her farewell, and then backed out of that tiny, U.S. Post Office in Keeler, California.

We picked up the pace as we followed a solitary dirt road that led due north out of Keeler. The hard, flat surface was welcome relief from the rock and gravel and chopped-up earth we'd become accustomed to, and we relished the fact that we could actually see where we were heading. From the looks of the distant landscape, it was going to be a full day of flat land: no canyons, no mountain ranges, no spines or hog backs, no dead-end gullies or drop-offs.

On the other hand, however, such obvious indicators were reason enough to be suspect, and by then it was practically our motto: when it gets easier, be cautious! In that respect, our start of that particular day was really no different than any of the others.

A couple miles from town and the road led past a number of dirt heaps that were a mixture of trash and earth, mostly pieces of metal scrap interspersed amongst infinite pieces of glass scattered everywhere. As the wind continued its drive from the northeast, we began to sense why that dumping ground was void of the most obvious. Why of course. No paper! The wind took good care of it. *But where does wind-blown paper go? Is there a mountain of paper trash somewhere that we don't know about? It's like tire-tread rubber. Where does it go?* And as we trudged along, I wrinkled my toes inside my boots and began to wonder where all that worn heel-and-sole rubber disappears to. Amazing what the mind conjures up.

Then, suddenly, the trash heaps began to resemble monuments like sculpted figurines. Millions of pieces of broken glass lay muted in the dusty earth, the result of a constant wind that blew across that primitive stretch of desert—and ahh, the many catsup bottles. Keelerites, or whomever, must have many sweet dreams and memories, and I'd keep those bottles in mind, since they would be grim reminders of how devastating that wind-dust could be. The bottles were etched and pitted; their surfaces had been exposed to the harassing winds of the Owens Valley, roughened and sanded as if having been blasted with a high pressure sand machine.

The heaps, the scrap, the glass, the bottles, smooth and pitted—a dichotomy of nature's best—with all kinds of weird angles that jutted skyward. The macabre, wind-swept landscape made us suddenly see and feel the effect of an outlaw wind that had nowhere to go except in all directions. It had nothing better to do than to blast an already taxed land and to batter the living beings who had lived and died in such a place. It was a different sense, a different scale.

The Sierras were closer than ever, and the dust clouds forming toward the southern part of the valley were getting bigger and closer!

The road ended. Not really ended, but just kind of disappeared as Jerry and I, mesmerized by days of thoughtless pace, suddenly realized it was behind us.

The dirt beneath us transformed into a hard-slab sand, and like overgrown boys with new toys, we joyfully discovered that we could make our boots squeak if we dug our toes in at just the right angle. Then, just like in Death Valley, the ground became uneven and tufts of wire grass and iodine bush began to show.

Off to our left, west, we caught our first glimpse of dark brown. It was mud! Real, wet mud that turned to a dull blue the further out you looked, and at the end of the blue were those clouds of dust: silt dust! And whereas before, we were satisfied that the wind was blowing in that direction—away from us—we weren't so sure then, as we suddenly realized that the wind-driven mass wasn't moving away from us! The dust was merely filling up the southern portion of the valley and not moving any further.

It was saturation! The huge brownish puffers were simply getting bigger in volume and it dawned on us, literally, that the whole valley was filling up with dust! We quickened our pace to stay ahead of the churning mass, and aimed for a piece of greenery that lay about a mile ahead of us. As we got closer, the verdant green seemed to merge into a larger slope of sand—a sand dune! By midday, as we approached even closer, it was evident that we were coming to a seep, a spring! Water!

We split an orange and a turnip, and then turned to our new-found water supply to supplement our lack of food. By golly, if we didn't have much to eat, we'd sure as hell drink!

Drinking our fill, and cradling our canteens, we hunkered down on the leeward side of the vegetation-locked sand dune for protection from the wind. Even with a fairly decent shelter, sprinkles of sand managed to find their mark as heavier gusts of wind roller-coastered over the top of the dune and down to where we huddled together. Even after drinking our fill of water, we still kept our canteens full. With other oncoming dust, we didn't know what we'd need in way of additional water. *What do you do in a dust storm anyway? Soak your head? Soak a shirt and wrap it around your face and head? That's it!* We soaked our lightest shirts, and, for the time being, we slung them like scarves around our necks. If it really got bad, we'd suck on loose ends; we would wet filter ourselves if all else failed.

The sun faltered and then, the dust fog was upon us. Only occasionally did the sun disappear completely, but our entire environment became dull and listless as the dirt, silt, and wind became our new world.

The brownish air didn't sting or abrade; no, it just filtered, and spread, succinctly, like a fine, swirling mist, dirty and nasty.

Our hair gradually thickened, and I began to notice Jerry's powdered beard, eyelashes, and brows. His glasses needed cleaning. He said to me finally, "You got dirty tears."

"Screw this!" I said, tersely, and then spat, defiantly. "Take me to the river!"

"Yo!" chimed Jerry, "To the river!"

We both began to cough and to clear our throats.

"No more talking," I said. "Cover up, suck water! Let's get the hell outta here!"

We filled our canteens one last time.

Jerry was already on the way. He turned once and hand-signaled to a series of telephone poles up ahead.

"Okay, okay," I thought to myself and hand-signaled for him to keep going, follow the poles! Yes siree! They'd lead to Lone Pine!

I followed Jerry, keeping him just within sight, and it seemed like hours of endless trudging as my eyes and throat began to burn—no exception for Jerry—as we followed the line of telephone poles that ran north and then northwest toward the northern end of Owens Lake. We stayed with the poles as they led away from the mud that drew further toward the middle.

Our whole day was hued into a light, dull tan as silt drifted in and out of our lives like mist, or steam, on a winter's day—or a hellishly hot day! Our day was somewhere in between. No, not cold like the 7,000 foot Malpais Plateau. No, not freezing like it would be at 13,000 feet, but a sweaty warm at our 4.000 foot elevation at the Owens Dry Lake Bed. Screw the dust!

Suddenly, it was right before us: a tree line! Big, bushy, low-cut trees! It was the Owens River!

We both saw the tree line through the haze at the same time; we broke to a trot, our packs clanging and groaning.

We pulled away our filter shirts. I vividly recall how Jerry looked just like the fictitious tank commander, fresh in from a hundred-mile dash across the Algerian deserts of Northern Africa. No, not Field Marshall Rommel, but Freeman!

We high-fived and shouted and hooted as we charged up over the final parapet like Marines at Iwo Jima, and finally looked down onto a body of water! It was the Owens River—slow and deep and full! *Water*!

Within minutes, we had our packs off, boots off, clothes off, and were heading for the water!

At the last minute, I grabbed Jerry's arm as he literally streaked by. "Hey man, can you swim?"

Jerry couldn't hold back his laughter. It was the funniest thing in the world to him, and dumb me, I was serious.

But there we were. Two grown men, somewhere in the Owens Valley, in a swimming hole, in a dust storm.

Glory be!

The trees that flourished along the shoreline of the Owens River helped considerably to repel the winds that still ravaged all around us. The weathered bluff that ran parallel with the river also helped as Jerry and I luxuriated in our first water bath in ten days. It was our own private beach that consisted of the base of the largest of the willow trees, a sloping, weed-covered foreshore, and just plain dirt!

The water was slow-moving, sluggish, but it wasn't stagnant. It was cool—not cold—and it cut away the grime, the sweat—even old pieces of Death Valley bog mud that somehow rode with us all the while.

Yet, we weren't filthy. We weren't scumbags! And what I mean by that—from a survivor's standpoint—is that if you should be without bathing water, and don't even consider soap, wash cloth, or towel, you simply let the wind and sunshine do the job. Take off your boots and socks, frequently. Swipe between the toes and let the air do the rest. Strip down, spread your legs, comb out the hairs, and let the wind and sun do the rest. Under your arms, the same way.

If you do have spare water, a cupful will do, always pour the water into your washing hand, and never dunk that hand; you'll contaminate the cup water itself. So, in that respect, the Owens River was a total bonus, a payback, or payoff.

While frolicking like young pups, we let our socks dry after giving them a water wash-rinse. We'd put them on wet, however, as we couldn't wait forever for them to dry completely. And that's okay, as you *can* wear wet clothing. Your own body's heat will do the drying. A damp sleeping bag? Get into it anyway and, again, let your body heat do the work. A soaked bag? Throw it under a tree shelter—or otherwise—or throw it over some bushes, or a small tree, and let it dry on its own; never throw it over a solid rock as it'll just rewet itself from its own condensation.

You're soaked, and without your bag, or other shelter? Dig a hole in the ground and cover yourself up with debris: dirt, sand, leaves, like a sand-hole at the beach. Even with cooking, all you need is a frying pan, a knife and spoon, and a cup. The cup is never put to the fire and all heating is done in the pan. When finished, don't wash it, or even rinse it out. *Lick* it out, or scrape-swipe it out with your fingers or tongue. They're your own germs, nobody else's, and you should be able to tolerate your own defense system, your own salivic enzymes. When you're finished, expose the eating part of your pan to open flame, then carry it on the outside of your pack.

And so it goes when taking care of yourself in the wild.

Repacked and ready to go, we knew what our next obstacle would be: getting to the other side of the river. At our location, it was like a small lake, maybe fifty to seventy-five yards across. Too big, too far out to work up a raft unless our lives depended on it, which was not the case. We were simply at the northern end of Owens Lake, practically at the very junction where the river fed into the main body of water. No wonder it was so wide.

We knew we had to keep heading north until the river was narrow enough to cross. How many miles? It was anybody's guess: twenty, thirty miles? That'd be way too far. We were aware that the highway that skirted Keeler was also up ahead, somewhere north of us. There'd have to be a bridge, eventually, at a specified point where the highway would begin its westward swing.

So, north it was. Back into the wind and dust looking for a bridge to get us on with our journey.

By late afternoon, the bridge came into sight. We crossed, feeling totally out of place, as if we'd somehow cheated to some degree. We had allowed the river to bring us to our knees; we caved in and went to the bridge. But in all candor, true survival is utilizing whatever is there, natural or the work of man! We took the bridge, rationalizing that we had done the right thing.

We weren't dumb. Stupid maybe, but certainly not dumb. Well, maybe on second thought…in our spare moments, we'd have to think about that.

The sun dropped away early, and why shouldn't it? The mighty Sierras were finally right in our laps, so to speak. They had the right to hide the sun whenever they wanted, as they had done so for millennia.

Even with the sun's disappearance, the wind kept up its relentless drive, but the closer we got toward the mountains—the closer to Lone Pine—the less airborne dust there was. The wind was cleaner, which meant we'd finally crossed the dust line that ran, dead center, north to south, through the very innards of the Owens Dry Lake Bed. The Indians, and early pioneers of Lone Pine, must've realized that: the closer one is, or was, to that eastern flank of the Sierra, the more shelter one had from the middle wind.

We felt that phenomena: the closer the Sierras, and the darker it got, and the fresher the wind, the more intuitive was the feeling that we were close to our final destination for the night—Lone Pine!

Immediately after leaving the bridge, just like before, it was back into the open desert, heading due west, into twilight.

"Yo, thar she blows!" shouted Jerry, finally.

We stopped and squinted.

"Yeah, man, I can see 'em!" I said as the oncoming darkness made it easier for us to finally pick out distant lights.

"Look, some of them are moving, it's the highway!" Jerry cupped his hand like it was a telescope and held it up to one eye.

Highway 395, the main overland route through the valley, was dead ahead, and slightly to our right by at least a couple miles was a cluster of still lights.

"Lone Pine! Damn, we're coming south," said Jerry, almost dejectedly.

"That's okay," I shot back, keeping up the enthusiasm, "we'll hit the Visitor Center south of town. That's the best place. It'll be perfect!"

"Yeah, yeah!" Jerry's voice suddenly perked up. "Yeah, that *will* be perfect, don't want to go into town."

In all seriousness, that's exactly what we didn't want: to go directly into town. No, no, no! We told Doyle to look for us from the highway, south. That would put us about where the Inter-Agency Visitor Center would be.

Jerry and I had both been at the Center many times, looking at books and such, in regard to the Sierras and the surrounding desert area. The facility was like a mini-museum, and you couldn't miss seeing it as you traveled the 395. Besides, the Visitor Center grounds were like a park. We'd camp there, *away* from the public!

There're no heroics in that kind of thinking. We simply wanted to keep to ourselves. We didn't want to have to explain to people what and who we were, why, how, and so forth.

Our mind-set wasn't with people at that point. It was like before a big game and we were operating under a different premise, a spectrum of intense thought and focus.

I could recall when I returned home from Korea with the 1st Marine Division. I didn't want to try and explain it; I kept it all in. Who'd understand anyway?

But the women in the desert, you say? The Saline Valley?

That was different. They saw us under *our* circumstances, *our* environment, *our* combat area!

But to go *into* Lone Pine, into a town environment, well, people would have a difficult time accepting us. We would've been homeless scumbags, no-account-good-for-nothings.

With our present attitude, we would've been disgusted, anyway, in having to deal with them, the opulence, the arrogance. People just wouldn't understand; they wouldn't have the foggiest as to what we were doing, or had done, or why?

Oh sure, you can read about such endeavors, and you can explain to people, if it's the right time and place, and if your *appearance* is up to public expectations at that right time and place. Then you could talk about it, show photographs, and offer the written word. That approach would be much more acceptable.

No, we'd complete our deed first; we'd rejoin society on our own terms, just let us come down.

It's the same when coming in from any long-term trek, especially so after having gone solo. "Please let me be, you'd not understand."

Who could possibly fathom what it's like to live like a Neanderthal? "Let me catch up, let me readjust, let me come down."

Let me write about it, distribute it, and then say, "Here, take some time. I can't tell you in ten minutes. Here. Read about it, digest it, think about it." Or, here, here are my photos, a thousand words!

Photographs, the written word, the verbal presentation after the fact. Powerful!

Yes, dead ahead, were dim, static lights just south of town. A fence, climb over, driveway, trees, the building, *the Visitor Center*! We were there: *Lone Pine!*

Food, food, food!!!

It was dark, and all the employees were gone for the night. We had the perfect spot. I mean, *perfect*! It was the entranceway to the Visitor Center. The facade faced west to east, and since the colder winds had shifted to that very direction, the entranceway made us the perfect shelter.

And Doyle? We had a feeling he'd be hanging around that general area, since the highway—the one that crossed the bridge that we traversed earlier—coincided with the north to south, Highway 395, right at the Visitor Center location. Sure enough, there came a flash-lighted figure across the field. It was Doyle walking toward us. He'd sighted us from the Visitor Center gate, after finally seeing us at the entranceway.

"Hey man," We bellowed, "Where's your pack? We got water *for you!*"

As you can imagine, the jokes went on and on. It was a fun time, a memorable occasion.

It was getting later and colder, and there was still work to be done. Obviously, Lone Pine was a very important juncture since it was our resupply point. It would be our staging area for the final push for Whitney, close to the last chapter.

Jerry and Doyle immediately went into conference as to where we—Jerry and I—were headed next; there were weather concerns and a number of options depending on just that.

Doyle had our winter tools: ice axes, crampons, and heavier gloves. Everything else would remain the same, as previously planned: same clothes, same tent, sleeping bags, and so on; we'd give up nothing to Doyle.

As scheduled, I put our food plan to work. Food for heavier weather and higher elevations, cold, winter-type foods, at least enough for the next four days: Spam, almonds, apples, carrots, oranges, cheese, powdered milk, chocolate, soup, crackers, canned chicken, raisins, noodles, and the like.

The food list went to Doyle, and when everything began to finally settle down, he went into Lone Pine. He was then the 'town man.'

When Doyle returned, Jerry and I met him at his truck to help carry back the new bags of food to our shelter at the entranceway.

Food! What a joy, and all we really cared about, at that moment, was getting supper started. There was no problem with water for drinking, or cooking. We had our own faucet right next to the porch.

But first, we returned to Doyle's truck to see him off. He would be heading for the 8,000 foot Whitney Portal area—our next day's destination.

"Hold on!" said Doyle as he walked back over to the cab of his truck. "I have a little something for you guys, the Lone Pine trophy!" He hauled out two cans of apricots and peaches, one of each.

"Here," he continued. "May the spirit be with you! It's your dessert, from the sugar-gods!"

"These are the most gorgeous cans I've ever seen," said Jerry, with a childish grin.

"You gotta nice pair, Doyle," I quipped, grinning and shaking his free hand, and accepting one of the cans of fruit with the other. "Shit, just like retirement!"

"This all we get?" chided Jerry.

"What's wrong with ice cream and beer?" I added. "Damn, Doyle, a man will starve with this kinda stuff!"

That kind of stuff would work well, with the banquet dinner planned for later that night back at the entranceway, our shelter.

It was truly a joyous night as we bid Doyle so long, and as we watched him hang a U-turn and head off toward town on Highway 395. Suddenly, out of the blue of the night, nostalgia swept me back to the blondes that we'd met out in the Saline Valley and how they'd offered grapes. Too bad they weren't there in Lone Pine that night.

The grapes that is.

We fired up our little stove and huddled in close, for warmth. We boiled pans full of water and worked up a packet each of macaroni and cheese; we split a can of corn, and ate the two cans of fruit Doyle gave us. We drank chocolate mixed with powdered milk and then poured the fruit syrup into some water and heated it up. That was the last event of the day before crawling, dead tired, into our sleeping bags.

There Must Have Been an Angel

The author (left) and Jerry Freeman at the lip of Rainbow Canyon after a 1500 ft. climb-out. (self-timed)

Jerry Freeman digs for water. Muddy water was as good as bottled water.

There Must Have Been an Angel

A rough bivouac deep in an unnamed canyon.
The author (foreground) Jerry Freeman at rear. (self-timed)

Sub-zero weather conditions on the way to Mt. Whitney.

A bit of civilization—old car bodies in Panamint Valley. The author (left) with Jerry Freeman (self-timed).

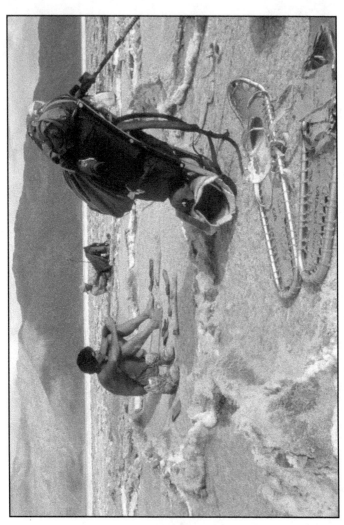

Using snowshoes to cross Death Valley's bogs. Author (left) with Jerry Freeman (self-timed).

There Must Have Been an Angel

The Whitney hut at roughly 40 below zero (windchill). Author (left) with Jerry Freeman.

Using rocks, Jerry Freeman digs for water in Rainbow Canyon.

There Must Have Been an Angel

At 110 degrees, the author (foreground) rests in available shade, Jerry Freeman (background). Note the tape on author's toes (self-timed).

Crossing Death Valley's notorious bogs, author (foreground), Jerry Freeman with binoculars.

The author coming off of Death Valley's bogs.

CHAPTER 11

DAY 11

Lone Pine, California

The night had been cold, but our concrete camp had been a welcome shelter since an even colder wind was still blowing, west to east. Again, the people who were familiar with the Lone Pine area, and its weather pattern, knew best where to situate the front door of such a facility, the Inter-Agency Visitor Center, lucky for us.

We were up before the sun, and from where we were, looking out toward the eastern desert, toward the direction of Keeler, the valley was clear of dust. Or were we witness to a new and refreshed wind cycle or pattern. Was this what looked like the start of a clear day only to have it fall apart, later on, with renewed wind and dust?

To hell with all of that! We'd paid our dues the day before when we finally worked our way out of the dust line. From here on though, the winds would be different: they'd be mountain winds, cold and biting, and not saturated with gawd-awful silt dust.

So it was with our new day, new sky, clear! Hard to imagine after such a dismal crossing from the day before, but the open heavens were in our favor, at least for the time being.

We were up and preparing to be on our way before any Center employees would show up. Our packs were considerably heavier with our renewed food larder, even though we would be carrying less in the way of a water supply. We were now in country we were familiar with, where water would be more abundant.

Our supper from the night before had been substantial. It was no less a class act as we fired up our trusty stove for our morning breakfast: Spam®, almonds, and an apple a piece, all cut up and mixed together in our frying pans, and heated to a smell-good morsel. It was a great treat!

We were ready to head on.

We crawled over the fence that separated the Center from Highway 395, and before we realized it, before it really had time to register, we were cast upon the world of civilization.

Cars and trucks whizzed by, and I suddenly flashed backed to the year 1963 when I was riding bicycle, cross-country. The side of the road, the berm, the crap and junk that'd been thrown from vehicles, it was all there: minuscule pieces of trash, bottle caps, cigarette butts, milk cartons, paper wrappings—regardless of the wind—and glass, always glass! And even more ubiquitous, beer and soda cans. All the accouterments of an overabundant society, all the stuff that nobody really sees, because it's everywhere. I thought to myself, *Why don't people dump this crap in their own yards, their own living rooms? Some probably do.*

There was the familiar smell of gasoline and diesel and the sight of billboards. Then, the small business shops and larger establishments, curbs, sidewalks and driveways, telephone lines, and power poles, all those hazards that people love to litigate over.

Next came the large, neon-lighted gas station, and 'Café and Eat' signs and motels. That was another kind of shelter, or survival for the millions, and just because they weren't doing what Jerry and I were doing, civilized people are no less struggling, but certainly at a more sedate level, on different terms.

Jerry and I were drifters by choice. We had the wherewithal to do so, and we had to keep that, utmost, in mind. We had to keep that perspective in balance.

As soon as we could, we crossed over and away from the side of the highway. We followed a circuitous route through a sparse, rural neighborhood that soon gave way to small-acre plots of land that revealed an abundance of fences and horses, tractors and old hay rakes, and older cars and pickups. Every once in awhile, and at a distance, we'd see someone out doing early morning chores, with jackets on, and it reminded us of the weather and how we were still in full clothes, instead of shorts and thin shirts.

We finally worked our way over to the Portal Road, which would eventually end at the lower flank of the Sierras at 8,000 feet, at Whitney Portal.

Doyle would already be up there. Not for a water drop, but because that would be the end of the line for him. He wouldn't be able to go any further unless, of course, he wanted to shoulder a pack and play the odds against the big mountain. We certainly didn't expect him to do that. No, his function was 'checkpoint,' and he had fulfilled that mission commendably.

We followed the road for less than a mile until it crossed over Lone Pine Creek. At that point, we finally broke away, and, once again, we were alone on the open desert. Portal Road continued on with its westerly course, Jerry and I headed away, slightly southwest, and that put us on the inside flank of the Alabama Hills.

The Alabamas have always reminded me of something very alien. The brownish-colored, oval shaped rocks seemed to be distressed as they lay in vast, jumbled heaps across a stretch of landscape somewhere between Lone Pine, proper, and the eastern edge of the Sierra Nevada Range. South to north, the outcropping began to show itself near Owens Lake and extended northward, and ended—abruptly—about ten miles past Lone Pine, at Hogback Creek.

As Jerry and I drifted away from the last remnants of country roadway, we found ourselves alongside those Alabama Easter Island-like, rock headstones. It was almost as if we were suddenly thrust into the very faces of Mount Rushmore. To see the Alabamas from a distance—from the roadway—was something in itself, but to walk and to move amongst such giants was an even more awesome experience.

We felt like exploring further, but we had no time; we just looked and allowed their very presence to almost intimidate. The ancient sculptures were watching; that was enough.

As we moved further west, those mammoth rocks finally stopped following, then they were behind us. There was nothing more between us—Jerry and I—and the Sierras!

There Must Have Been an Angel

By noontime, the savory, early morning desert smells were history. The aroma by then was low mountain. It was similar, in likeness, to our own desert at home, the Mojave! Every year, at about the same time, October and November, the crisp smells of fall would become heavy. It's as if the seeds of life were eager to burst, as in the first storm. That would relieve it all; it would be the announcement of a new term: winter! Once winter seeds were sown, the quietude of rain and snow would prevail, then the smells would change once again, it would no longer be fall.

It was familiar to Jerry and me, and the recall of the years spent in that part of the country were at their strongest as we trudged along, side by side—but alone—in silence, knowing full well that we were about to enter another vast region of superior mightiness.

Yes, we had endured the desert harshness, and in the past, had endured the mountain ruggedness, but at that moment, it was different, very different. Winter was coming!

And like the desert and its ungodly heat and lack of water, it'd now be the high mountains, plenty of water, plenty! But it'd be frozen! Oh, the lessons the pioneers must've learned.

So, take your pick. The multitude has already done so. Look where the towns are. Where are the people? Why, where it's easiest to survive, of course. Who in their right mind would settle in the heart of a desert or at the top of the highest mountain? Only fools.

Governments govern the towns and their people, nature dictates all the rest. It rules with an iron fist and allows no mercy for the few who refute even the most basic of rules: nature's rules!

Membership comes with a price, there are dues.

The air was still, and the temperature so comfortable that we nodded off during a rest break somewhere betwixt napping and deep sleep and being awake. Once again, the realization that fatigue always demands a payback was evident, but that's what's expected when one stops all of a sudden. It's like slugging up a dam in front of a huge wave, a motion of excitement and activity. Suddenly, you throw on the brakes, and wham! Everything comes to a halt!

Fatigue began to overwhelm us, and we began to see lizards lying about on the rocks, and we began to see us in them, and how we didn't even see as much as a lizard in Death Valley, too damned hot! No water! No shade!

We had stopped at the end of a dirt road at a large rock outcropping that we'd sighted from a distance. It was a perfect stopping point, almost as if it were a natural junction, and I was sure that many an Indian had stopped there before, in times past, while traveling between the high mountains and desert. The duration of the stopover would've depended on what time of year it was, especially if it were a water rock.

I looked closely to see if there wasn't a depression, or bowl, somewhere along the hard surface that would've held rainwater. There was nothing. It was just a rock. A rest rock.

We'd pulled off our boots and socks, and, once we'd rested a bit, we took lunch: an orange a piece, and banana chips. We knew water was up ahead.

We were resting, and had just about finished lunch, when seemingly out of nowhere, a pickup truck appeared, coming slowly down the road. There wasn't a lot of dust, but just a drift to indicate a slower speed.

At about thirty yards, the truck passed by, the driver nodded and kept going.

"That wasn't normal, Jerry. That guy wanted to stop."

"That wasn't Forest Service was it?" he asked in return.

"Truck wasn't right," I said, "but the guy looked official, no uniform though."

We were low to the ground, below the sage line, and we weren't able to track the truck, nor did we want to jump up and become obvious. We continued with lunch.

Suddenly, the truck reappeared from the last-seen direction. The driver stopped a short distance from us, got out, and walked toward us.

Shit! I thought to myself. *Here we are barefoot, and we got some stranger comin' in on us. At least there's two of us, and the man's not showing a weapon. He's turned the motor off, he's got the keys.*

"Howdy," he said, casually, non-threateningly.

"How ya doin'?" I returned, Jerry nodded.

"Been out long?" he asked.

"Long enough, going on...," I turned to Jerry. "What is this? Our eleventh day?"

"Eleven days," replied Jerry, matter-of-factly.

"You wouldn't happen to be Bergthold, or Freeman, coming from Death Valley?"

"Well, I'll be damned." I stood, and nodded toward Jerry, "Jerry Freeman, I'm Lee, Lee Bergthold."

"Hi-Tec's® looking for you guys," continued the man, "the boot company out of Modesto."

"Well, I'll be damned," I repeated. "You mean someone actually misses us?"

Jerry and I laughed, the man smiled.

"Yeah, we know Hi-Tec," said Jerry, then standing. "Dave Pompel, we got their boots!" Jerry held up a battered, oatmeal-colored boot: "Hi-Tec, yeah, we know 'em!"

I nodded to my own pair on the ground, next to me: "thread-bare and a little dirty, but they've done well."

Jerry broke off a dried piece of Death Valley bog mud off one of his boots and tossed it to the man. "The bogs, Death Valley, mean shit! They made it through!"

The man smiled and then chuckled. "Anyway, Dave Pompel at Hi-Tec called and he was wondering if you'd made it this far, obviously you have. They knew you were heading this way, you're using their boots."

"We made it okay," I said. "So did Patagonia® and North Face and Peak-1."

Jerry moved up to my right side. "We used snowshoes on the bogs," he said, "Stowe®, out of Vermont!"

"So we heard," the man replied. "Oh, by the way, I'm Art Gaffrey, District Ranger for this area." He offered his hand.

We exchanged, all around.

As the dialogue continued, we talked about the overall trek, itself, but, more specifically, the bogs crossing, water (and the lack thereof), our equipment, and the time of the year, and finally: the weather! And Mt. Whitney!

"You men look pretty well adapted to what you're doing. Did you know that we've got a pretty heavy storm system coming in?" Art Gaffrey nodded toward the north, toward the clouds that were just beginning to show over the northwestern part of the distant peaks.

He continued, "Ordinarily, we issue a stern warning to people heading for Whitney, especially this time of year, but you men look as if you can take care of yourselves."

"We're sure as hell not complacent about it, the weather and all," said Jerry. "We know it can kick the crap out of us, we're not heroes."

"Your feet okay?" asked Gaffrey, noticing the taped parts and Moleskin® on our feet.

"We don't like blisters," I said. "We tape the hots 'fore they take off on us."

"How 'bout your hand?" Gaffrey glanced at Jerry's taped thumb and finger.

"Just a scratch, it's okay." Jerry flexed his hand.

"Pretty solid, you guys, levelheaded. Of course, you can't always judge a man by the looks of his pack, but from the looks of *those* packs, I'd say you been around awhile." Gaffrey's official nature was beginning to show.

"We been there," I said, wryly. "We know, no chances, no heroics, we just go 'til it turns us back, that's all we can do, want to see our permit?"

The sudden change of subject, and the relief of such a last statement, was comical. All three of us laughed.

"Just because we got this marriage license doesn't mean it's gonna be a rose garden."

"Waddaya mean we can't die on your mountain? We got this permit!"

There was more good-natured laughter as we all shook hands once again.

Art Gaffrey walked back to his truck, he waved so-long as he headed back in the direction of Lone Pine.

Watching his truck disappear down the road was very much like watching Doyle drive away after leaving us water. Gaffrey had also left us something, something to ponder. It was like an omen, almost subliminal. "I see you have ice axes and crampons, you'll need 'em!"

Jerry and I went back to finishing our lunch and enjoying the warm sunshine. It then suddenly dawned on me that the name Gaffrey meant more than just what was exchanged at our chance meeting. Just a month prior—September, '89—the Mt. Whitney Ranger District had mailed me a Special Public Service award plaque for being instrumental in the locating and recovery of a jet aircraft canopy from the Olancha-Monache area, just south of Mt. Whitney. The plaque hangs on my wall at home. It's signed by Art Gaffrey, we had never met before.

From 'the rock,' we headed slightly southwest, toward Inyo Canyon. By mid-afternoon we came upon our first running water, other than the Lone Pine Creek that we passed over earlier that day.

We took a welcome break from our packs, and, on all fours—hands and knees—drank our fill of water from the tiny stream that tumbled, downward, from the rugged canyon of Inyo.

We were in deep, open shade by then at about 6,500-feet elevation, at about three in the afternoon. That meant cold! That meant heavier shirts and trousers, and yes, we were aware of the clouds that had begun to build from earlier on. But from our viewpoint—up against the eastern Sierra flank—it was difficult to see what the overall weather prospect was in relation to what we were doing. However, the words of Art Gaffrey had definitely put us on the alert: "...storm front coming!" That possibility was nothing new to us, and ever since Keeler, in relation to the Sierras, there's *always* the possibility of a storm coming!

Regardless of the distant clouds or the chill, there was an effervescent beauty—almost a mystique, if you will—that seemed to engulf us at that creek crossing. Even though the landscape was basically high desert, the water source had created a magical garden of verdant plant life. It included different species of fern and vine, along with a golden-green mantle of leaves that lined the tiny creek bed.

Over the years, the both of us had seen and experienced the driest of deserts, only to come upon lush, jungle-like corridors where water was suddenly abundant. So dense were some of those spots, you'd swear you were in the outback of New Guinea or an Amazonian rain forest. The crossing at the head of Inyo Canyon was no exception.

Within yards of such a lush environment, it was back to the dryness of desert, but not entirely. Scrub brush and even smaller species of pine finally made their debut as the elevation increased, along with the cold.

The old, unused road we were following—the original Portal Road—eventually turned into a maintained trail, and, the better maintained it became, the closer we knew we were to the actual Whitney Portal.

Finally, as the day slowly transformed its way into dusk, and with the sounds of Lone Pine Creek nearby, we arrived at our night's destination.

Doyle had positioned himself where he figured we'd show, we were all on target: Doyle at the end of the main road and Jerry and I at the end of the old road.

With barely enough light left in the day, and with another set of miles down and behind us, Jerry and I set about in search of firewood to bolster what Doyle had already gathered.

Using large rocks as a breaker, we broke up the longer lengths of wood into smaller, pit-size chunks. Since the wood was down and dry, the pieces splintered with relative ease. We soon had a stack of firewood for that night's warmth and dinner.

Obviously, the darkness of night lowered the air temperature, but since we were finally in amongst timber, we would have considerable protection from the cold or if the wind should decide to blow. On the other hand, the still air would guarantee a freezing night, regardless of the trees—but it was better than barren rock, and, from what I could see, straight up through the trees, the sky was clear. That was another sign that it would be even colder. The clear weather was encouraging.

We set up our tent—Doyle would use his truck—then we scooped out a simple hole for our fire. Since we were in the woods, and there was the possibility of bears, even though it was cold, we hung a bear rope. We drew water and then went to a cold night schedule: remove boots, socks and insoles, place under a slanted rock. If the air—the weather—is dry, then hang the socks on a limb or branch to air out. Once again, not on solid rock, as the socks would just sweat back into themselves; put on fresh socks with tennis shoes, give our feet a break.

Next, put on thermals: tops and bottoms, long trousers next, baggy is best, I use heavy-duty camos. Then, two sweatshirts, the top one with a high, zip-up collar. Last, is a light-weight, thermal jacket with hood.

Around the neck? Balaclava, with a watch cap underneath, everything on top the head and over the ears. Gloves, yes! If it rains: poncho and chaps, additional. Nighttime: food, counterhang (bear rope), everything else in pack, cover pack with poncho, rock it down, rope and rock down tent if there is wind.

The regimen above is what I considered basic and essential for standard 10,000 to 13,000 foot elevation—summer! The regimen is the same for the desert—winter! Cardinal rule: stay out of the desert mid-summer and stay out of the high mountains mid-winter! And what about our situation? I reiterate: hit Death Valley as late as you can to avoid the blistering summer heat, get to Whitney before the first snow.

How were we measuring up in regard to that plan?

Well, and I looked up to the sky once again: clear, so far, stars, cold!

The first and only fire was a definite comfort. The water was the freshest, and the dinner was the greatest: fried potatoes with onion and garlic. We had cheese and chocolate with powdered milk, and a half piece of squash, each.

We sat in silence around the last of the fire, and my thoughts rambled as I glanced at Jerry's bearded and tanned face. His hands showed rough in the firelight, as he knelt forward to warm them. His clothes were color-dulled from years of wear, from sun, and rain, and wind. I glanced at my own tennis shoes and at the holes, on top, with my sweat socks sticking through. My hands, too, were roughened, and lined, and veined, and my stubbled face felt like a horse brush.

My jacket—the zipper was stuck a third of the way down—had frayed cuffs and duct tape patches; my trousers were still with whitish stains from Death Valley dirt and dust.

My balaclava was new—Patagonia! My watch cap, however, had a big hole in it.

Suddenly, I began to consider the fact that maybe—just maybe—our gear might not be sufficient for 13,000 and 14,000 foot work, not for that time of the year, anyway, and especially so, if we were to confront a fierce winter storm!

I also considered the fact that, for years, I had always carried the same bindle, cold or hot, rain or shine, winter, or summer. My stuff would have to hold one more time.

I began to think about my kids, and my closest friends back home, and how I couldn't desert them or disappoint them, I was committed.

I thought about Art Gaffrey: *"Ice axes and crampons!"*

I thought about Doyle, we couldn't have done it without his support. I was glad that he and Jerry were brothers. They had a stake in each other, I had a stake in both of them.

I rose to get away from the glare of the firelight. I wanted to look up through the trees one more time before crawling into my sleeping bag.

Stars? Wait!

"Jerry, Doyle! Come over here! You guys see stars?"

There were none! Clouds had moved in!

"Holy shit!" I mumbled.

"No big deal," replied Jerry, solemnly, his warm breath showing steam from the backlit fire, at a distance. "It'll just get warmer."

"You joker, you." Doyle was gripping his coffee cup.

We chuckled, and then shuffled back to the fire.

CHAPTER 12

DAY 12

Whitney Portal

During the night, the clouds had moved in, thus keeping the temperature at a more tolerable level. It was actually warmer on that twelfth morning than it had been the night before, and, with the overcast plus the additional foliage—trees, creek brush, and the like—the increased humidity made it feel like a foggy morning along the coast.

Although it was no surprise for us to feel the added moisture, there was a heaviness in the air at Whitney Portal. It wasn't just the overcast, per se. No, it was more like an omen of a distant wet storm coming, as opposed to a dry, cold air mass that could produce snow and ice!

Like other past mornings, we packed in silence as the lingering smoke from our fire drifted hazily throughout the small clearing. The acrid smell was all too familiar, and in its own way, it was friendly, soothing. We scurried about, each of us holding to our own thoughts.

I knew we were concerned and thinking about the same thing: the weather! Accompanying those crucial thoughts, we were at least relieved that our water supply would no longer be a problem. We nonchalantly coined a new buzz phrase: "Suck Ice!"—just for the hell of it—a subliminal kick in the butt to get us going that morning.

"Yo! Suck ice!" one would shout.

"Yo! Suck ice!" would be the reply.

We thought it had a nice ring to it. Obviously, we were easily entertained. We went about our business of loading up.

I deftly swung my ice ax at the air just to get the feel of the weight, and to reassure my confidence in my own strength.

"Yo! Chop! Suck ice!" I swung again and again. I stopped midair, took a deep breath, then inspected the tip. Satisfied, I strapped the ax onto the back of my pack under the outside bungee cord, my crampons would fit on the outer sides of each side of the pack, under the same cord.

I let the cord snap a second time, then a third. Something wasn't quite right. Then it dawned on me, but it still wasn't clear enough. What was wrong? What was bothering me?

I was drawing blanks, mentally. Was I was still asleep? *No, no! I'm awake! I'm tired! No, and no!* Again, *I'm strong, fresh! No, there's weakness!*

Was it the weather? Was the trek over? Was a storm going to stop us? Were we going to quit?

No! Yes! Maybe.

I leaned back and felt the cold of the ground as it suddenly permeated from underneath. *Never sit directly onto the cold, exposed ground,* I thought to myself. *Oh, how the body draws the cold, like a sponge.*

I looked over toward Doyle and watched him load his truck; Jerry was doing the same as I was, strapping on his ice ax and crampons. He let one of his cords snap.

I smiled to myself, let my head nod. *I know what it is, I do, I do. It's Whitney itself!*

I rose and walked over to Jerry.

"Yo, Jerry! I know what it is!"

"Know what *what* is?"

"I know what's draggin' us this morning."

"Yeah, know what you mean. Must be the weather."

"No," I said. "That's only part of it."

"Might snow!" he returned.

"I know, I know. But look at the parking lot. Nobody's here." I gestured toward Doyle's truck. "There are only two other cars here. Hell, the place is deserted. You know what it's like here in the summer? There'd be five-hundred people here." My hands were suddenly cold; I blew into them and marveled at how my breath turned to steam. "Whitney's no big deal," I continued. "Thousands have climbed it, but how many go up it in a storm? It's the same old story: if it's easy, they'll do it. Tough, everybody goes home."

"You got that straight," replied Jerry. "Like a blizzard! This sky is heavy duty; it's gotten still, something's going on. Screw it!" He looked up, smiling. "Ain't it beautiful?"

"That's the point, exactly," I declared, excitedly. "That's the spirit, damned if it isn't! That's why we're here, man!"

The night before, when we realized that clouds were moving in, we discussed the possibility that the trek could be over if it really turned crappy. That underlying feeling of defeat was still dominant come morning.

But the come down was more than just one factor plus another. It was a combination of several: the incoming weather, and the possibility of a total blowout; Whitney, itself, and its lofty 14,000-plus height, *and our gear and equipment.* Could we withstand the severity of a major storm at that altitude? If we *should* get to the top, would we be able to return, or would we be blocked in? How bad is the ice further up? Is anyone else up there? How far?

The *real* truth was the fact that Jerry and I would be reluctant to turn back just because of the weather. We'd never made a habit of turning tail. *Did the pioneers turn back? Did they even have that option?*

Pride. That's what it was, instinctive pride. We weren't used to quitting. We'd always worked it out, always! And yet, it was unsettling. How bad would it have to get before we would even consider packing it in? Would we push too far, beyond the point of no return?

Yeah, man, that's why we're here.

Our commitment of the past days—as would always be the case—had been a mixture of enthusiasm, excitement, and curiosity in the crossing and exploration of a raw land that few, if any, would ever set foot upon. Places like Lone Pine and Whitney Portal, why, you could drive right to them. There's a trail up Whitney, just follow it, damn, people even run up it!

We figured that crossing the desert to Lone Pine would have been our major challenge. Anybody with reasonable determination could have gone on from there. But suddenly, from out of the blue—literally—and with the possibility of the season's first major storm moving in, *our* situation had begun to change, radically. The change didn't take us by surprise, but our frame of mind just hadn't gotten quite up to speed. We hadn't been concerned with an ending. We simply accepted the fact that the mountain would be there, waiting. All we had to do was climb to the top. That would be our *coup de grace,* our final stroke!

But a storm? It was akin to a race that had come down to the wire. We thought we had it whipped, as it were. *We're slipping! We're falling behind, someone's gaining, we've allowed ourselves to become complacent. Come on, let's get our asses in gear!*

The summit of Mt. Whitney would officially be the end, but we had to get there first, before we could rule. And then, we'd have to come down. We would still have to get *off* the mountain, and there was a storm not too far away. Yes, the situation had definitely taken a change.

Was the trek over? Not by a long shot!

"Okay," said Jerry. "We know where we're going; we've been there before. Let's head for Outpost Camp and check it out. If it's clear, we move up, simple as that."

"Hold it!" I replied. "Trail Camp is 12,000. Too far. It's exposed! If we get that far, we may as well shoot for the 13,000 crest and on up. I like the idea of at least getting to Outpost by dark. There's still some shelter there."

"Okay, I'll buy that," continued Jerry. "If we get hit there, that's where the shelter is, trees 'n stuff, even some brush, as I recall."

"Yeah," I said, rubbing my hands and pulling down tightly on my balaclava. "Make sure we get a straight shot and do it all at once: Tail Camp, 13,000, and then shoot for the top, that's savvy!"

"Rope!" said Jerry.

"Check!" I said.

"Crampons, ice ax."

"Check!" I said, as I carried my pack over next to Jerry's.

Doyle, not far from us, was still loading items into the back of his truck. He could overhear our conversation, but he had been unusually quiet, until "…now wait a damn minute here," he said, matter-of-factly. Walking toward Jerry and me he continued, "I don't want to see you guys taking no chances."

"Oh crap! Here comes the Sparklett's Man," mumbled Jerry as he still worked with his pack. "Not water he's worried about, though."

"Well, he's concerned," I said to both of them, as Doyle walked up.

"Damn straight, I am," Doyle repeated. And his concern *was* genuine.

Even when crossing the desert, Doyle—the Water Man—had held steadfastly to his post, waiting, waiting, waiting. Now, with the final end in sight, it was obvious he didn't want to be witness to any screw-ups.

"I *am* concerned," repeated Doyle. "The desert heat and no water was one thing, this cold is another. This high altitude, the cold, I don't know about this."

"No, no!" I said. "No chances, that's not the case. We just work it out like always. No chances. Hell, I don't wanna come outta here an ice ball!"

Doyle chuckled. "Ice ball, fire ball, you guys oughta be somewhere in between. Hell, what's wrong with a motel in Lone Pine?"

We laughed.

"That'll be the day," snorted Jerry.

"No shit!"

"Yeah, just like an iron horse."

"A mighty *big* iron horse," one of us said.

"Now, if there's women down there…"

"That would really put us over the top; talk about comin' back in a basket."

"That's the only way to look at it," said Jerry finally. "We still got work to do, we just keep going as far as we can. If it snows ten feet, well then, we might reconsider."

"Exactly!" I said.

"I don't know," said Doyle, pacing in a circle. "I just don't want you guys gettin' into something you can't get out of."

"No, don't worry," said Jerry. "You know us better than that. You know how safety conscious this guy is?" He pointed directly at me. "He wanted to know if I could swim down at the river. Can you imagine that?" Jerry laughed, we all did.

"How'd I know if you could swim? Or couldn't? Damned if I was gonna carry you out. I already had a load!"

"Yeah, but you coulda had the food!" chided Jerry.

"Don't think I wasn't keepin' that in mind."

"I got bacon 'n eggs in the truck. Too bad you guys can't have any."

"Get outta town, Doyle! Your life's in jeopardy!"

We laughed and shuffled around a bit. We all had mixed feelings.

"We go 'til we can't," reiterated Jerry.

"Agreed," I said.

"Okay," said Doyle. Laughingly, he pointed a finger at me. "That's my brother you got out here."

"Bullshit! That's my partner! Just like my brother!" Doyle and I shook hands. It was spontaneous, as if we were somehow reassuring each other. "We'll do okay, Doyle."

"You've come to be almost a brother, too. What'd you say your name was?" joked Doyle.

"We're all brothers," piped up Jerry.

"No, no," I said, lamenting. "Asshole buddies, simple as that. It's like a chain: we're the three links. It's got to be together, all or none. We couldn't have done this without Doyle, and *you* wouldn't have been here if it weren't for fools like *us*. How'd you get conned into this, anyway?"

"I told him we'd pay him," joked Jerry.

"What?! Pay! Damn it, the guy's on vacation! Look at all those lakes the guy's been to."

"You mean all those friggin' dry things back there?" Doyle spilled his coffee as he swung around to point toward the desert.

"He ain't heavy, he's my brother," quoted Jerry.

"Oh thank you Father Flannigan," I said heartily. I turned to Doyle. "Doyle, you're a sweetheart; it's worked out well. We'll be cool, we'll take it easy."

"Yeah, *cool* all right," said Doyle.

"We'll be okay," Jerry said again. "We'll hang in there."

"A toast!" I said suddenly, as I pulled my ice ax from my pack. I extended it outward. "A toast!"

"Yo! Suck ice!"

"Yo! Suck ice!" we chanted, as we toasted with two ice axes and an empty coffee cup.

"Hope nobody's looking," said Jerry, sheepishly.

"Who cares?" said Doyle. "Asshole buddies!"

"Partner!" I nodded to Jerry. "Checkpoint!" I nodded to Doyle.

We left Doyle behind.

It felt strange to be following a trail. Information gleaned from the few day hikers in the area indicated heavy ice further up.

We knew the trail would be good for only so far, and then we'd simply have to take a look for ourselves and see what the situation was like firsthand, then work it out from there. We would use the trail as long as we could.

Years ago, I learned that secondhand information was always to be taken with caution. What seemed tough to one person might not be so to another; it would always come down to the experience and background of the one giving the information.

While guiding others for many years, it was always interesting to hear the complaint, "How tough this is!" Eventually, they'd get into an even stiffer situation that would make the original scenario a piece of cake. It all goes back to the axiom, "I complained about having no shoes, 'til I saw a man with no feet!"

I would think about that in the days to come.

We were fully clothed except for thermals and gloves. With the extended energy due to the climbing and rise in elevation, we knew we would stay warm enough, at least for the time being.

We began our climb at 8,000 feet; we had to go to 14,495! It was almost November, it was cold, and the sky was heavy.

Within the hour, in crossing our first water outlet, we realized that the icing reports were dead-on. The tiny sub-creek was frozen solid!

We took a break to check the area further. We wanted to take a look at a series of falls that were always a feature during the warm months. And, since it had been a number of years since either one of us had been on the Whitney Trail, we weren't familiar with where the cataract-like falls were along Lone Pine

Creek. We knew that they were situated slightly to the south of us. We listened for the rush of water, but didn't detect any sound.

We soon found out why. The falls were frozen solid! I mean solid!

It wasn't that we didn't expect it, it just came as a surprise.

"You know what, Jer?" I said. "I think it's winter! What do you say?"

Jerry chuckled. "My good man, that is profound!"

And the first snowflake fell.

We knew we were both grappling mentally with the idea that the whole trek plan had just done a gigantic flip-flop. My thoughts rambled. *Come on! We've got to reset our focus. Get with it! Think cold! Winter!*

We gradually came to grips with a renewed mind-set.

"We haven't even started up this mountain, and already our water supply is down the tubes, literally!" said Jerry.

"Hell, we see ice all the time, even in summer," I replied, flippantly. "No big deal. So, it's frozen tight! So, we do *suck ice*."

"Screw the ice," said Jerry, not too enthusiastically. He paused. "Ah, this is great. Are we havin' fun yet?"

"Yes, my dear partner, we are having fun."

"Where's Doyle when you need him?" quipped Jerry.

"Yo, Doyle! Yo! Up here!" I joked. "We lost our water."

And more snowflakes began to fall.

"Just stare up at the sky and open your mouth. There's all kinds of water comin' down," said Jerry.

"God's dandruff. That's what it is."

We stood in complete silence in respect and awe of the frozen water that loomed vertically, before us, the snow continued to fall.

The snow fell off and on, light to heavy, clear one minute, flurries the next. The air was still, however, which made it seem ominous. It was like a loaded gun—we didn't know when it would go off. It created a strange mixture of excitement and caution. It was as if we wanted to drop bread crumbs to find our way back, let's not stop, but let's not go too far, either, let's keep a safety line!

And, like the canyons before, our psyches went into overdrive: *What if we can't get out at the end? Can we get back?*

We returned to the trail, and continued up. We climbed in silence—as always. If we could talk, we weren't working hard enough—our philosophy. Like running, if you've got enough energy to talk to a partner, you're simply not working hard enough.

We were usually one behind the other—or flanked out at a considerable distance—or we would be in such rough terrain that what little talk there was, was focused on the task at hand. "Put your left hand here! Your right hand there."

In our immediate situation, there was one other factor: altitude! Even as conditioned as we were, breathing became more difficult. No doubt about it, we were going up! In working with Jerry over the years, I knew that altitude affected him to a degree, but never to the point that it became a major problem, it just slowed him down a bit.

I was more fortunate. Altitude had never bothered me. Therefore, in spite of my age, I still excelled in long-haul, high altitude situations. This particular attribute was definitely in my favor as a matter of payback, or push-'n-pull, in regard to Jerry.

He was the pivot man; he excelled in rough terrain, straight-up-and-down high places, like cliffs, places where I, admittedly, felt fear.

It was a matter of one team member picking up the minor short-comings of another. It was a simple, ready-made checks-and-balance system, an important point in working with a partner.

So, in silence we worked, another long day, like so many of the others, one step at a time.

Another hour, two, three. The terrain became sparse; the rugged landscape took on a moon-like appearance as we gradually worked the upper fringes of timberline. The air became crisper, but we were warm from our own body heat and the increased upgrade.

Finally, looming in front of us, at a distance of roughly two miles, we caught our first glimpse of the exposed eastern wall of lower Whitney! It was majestic, foreboding, and beckoning, daring us to come closer.

Even at our distance, the vertical mass of ravaged rock looked depressed, rejected! After all, it had seen thousands of climbers over the seasons; climbers that struggled at the steepness and the circuitous switchbacks. But they'd quit coming. The climbers had gone home. After all, it was winter-like, snow was on the way.

The wall was powdered with white and we were glad of the distance between it and us. A low shrouded ceiling of grey hovered across the upper ridges; it was obviously snowing heavily. Jagged struts of black rock showed through as outcroppings—there was no top, no sky!

Outpost Camp was going to be our destination for the night. After seeing what was ahead, there would be no disagreement. Our limitations for that day had suddenly been ordained.

The few remaining pine trees offered less and less shelter as we climbed even higher. We figured that the wall up ahead was probably the 11,000 to 12,000 foot cut-off. Trail Camp would be just below that area, or at the base. Trail Camp is known for its last usable water during summer months—frozen, of course, during the winter. There was no more shelter after that. In fact, there would be little shelter at Trail Camp.

We ate lunch by one of the few remaining trees on the edge of timberline. The peanuts, raisins, and prunes were welcome, but the standing—we didn't want to sit on cold rock—soon chilled us. We tried sitting on the edges of our packs, but that didn't offer much warmth, either, since it cramped our legs and the warm air trapped inside our trousers was squeezed out.

Snow began coming down at a good rate. The trees, in that respect, made a decent shelter, though it had no significant affect on the temperature that was rapidly dropping.

To our astonishment, two men suddenly came into view; they were heading our way, down trail.

It was awkward for us to be in contact with other people; we barely spoke to the few we'd seen earlier at the Portal trailhead. Doyle had been our spokesperson. He did the talking to glean information, and so on.

But, these two men were actually a welcome sight. They had information about further up the trail, and, in turn, were eager for information from us. They had read and heard about two trekkers going from Death Valley to Whitney—us! And that, of course, opened up a lively discussion.

We became engrossed in an all-out verbal exchange even to the point of putting lunch on temporary hold. The payback, unfortunately, was that everyone got colder by the minute, including lunch—the result of just standing around.

The long and the short of the whole affair, however, was information. The two men had gotten as far as Trail Camp. They weren't equipped or experienced to go farther. Nonetheless, they gave us a report, "Heavy ice ahead, snowing off and on, no wind at the time, switchbacks—from Trail Camp on—not even discernible because of heavy icing. Two Brits and maybe two other climbers bivouacked at Trail Camp, supposedly day trekking, nobody else around, cold! Very cold!"

We thanked one another, and the men continued on their way toward the Portal. In the meantime, practically running in place to generate warmth, Jerry and I hurriedly finished our much colder lunch. We packed and prepared to move up, but first, we headed for a brush clearing to try to get water from the creek.

We ice-axed chips and shavings into our bottles. There was no time—or desire—to melt the tiny shards of ice and frost right then. We crunched and ate what we could, knowing full well we would lower our body temperature—always a tough call during cold weather since the body still needed vital hydration.

We decided to get water, farther up the trail, when we had more time for setting up the stove to melt the ice, but with everything turning white and our surroundings becoming darker by the minute, we only wanted to move—and fast!

It must have been close to three or four o'clock in the afternoon when we finally arrived at what we took to be Outpost Camp, or Outpost Meadow. Our topo map didn't delineate all the details for that area. Regardless of our actual location, that was as far as we would be going for that day.

As for the actual time, it felt much later than it was, since it was practically dark. The snowfall had temporarily ceased, but the cloud cover was so close it was like being in a fog, but not so dense as to be considered a whiteout.

Our main concern was warmth, not exploration, so we never looked for an actual meadow. We were well aware that the temperature would continue to drop as nighttime quickly approached.

Momentarily staring at the ground, I noticed that the fresh powder was separating itself from the old snow that had accumulated. The symbolism of old men versus the new kids on the block struck me. The *new* adding to the *old*, the old having that much more depth, exposure, and having had seen more of life, such as it was. The old patches were frozen solid, steadfast; the new were still fresh and soft enough to be scraped up, molded, and shaped into form.

Quickly, I shook my head. *Come back, come back! You're here now, there's work to be done!*

I saw the snow for what it really was. It would be our drinking water—Black Mountain Whiskey we called it, as melted snow always had a strange and bizarre taste, new and fresh and wintery.

"Hey! Look over here!" I yelled to Jerry as I backed up to a large rock to slip out of my pack. "It's one of those so-called solar toilets. I'll be damned!"

Appearing from out of the gloom was a toilet similar to ones we'd seen, at a distance, down lower, near the trailhead, an unexpected addition.

"Yep, that's what they got up here now, I guess," said Jerry, authoritatively, "like a town."

We hurriedly walked over to the small, chalet-type structure that looked like a miniature snow cabin.

"Damn! Like a small house," I declared. "Can you fathom that? A shelter!"

Carefully, because of ice, we walked up the slick wooden stairway. A door to the left was padlocked; the right door was unlocked, it *was* a toilet!

"Whoo-wee!" I chirped. "Look at this, Jerry! Home away from home, a shelter! A roof! We could live in this place!"

"We?" said Jerry, with a comical look on his face. "*We?*"

"Hell yes, *we*!" I replied enthusiastically. "Smell's not gonna hurt you. Look, one bag here, the other here, kinda squished up, legs over the stool, lid down, of course."

"Of course, my good man," replied Jerry. "Lid down, lid down, I'll take the tent!"

"Ah, come on now, Jer. There's room for both of us. I've slept in worse. It'll work! It's almost warm in here, almost."

Jerry stuck his head out the door. It was almost dark; it was cold! He quickly shut the door. Suddenly, it was dark inside.

"I'll tell you what," he said. "I know my bag's heavier than yours. By the way, when you gonna upgrade your gear? What is it, the 1920s?"

"I know, I know, I'm attached. I've had my stuff a long time, old buddies."

"Yeah, attached all right," said Jerry. "Yer gonna freeze to death one of these nights."

"Not tonight, man! I'm gonna sleep in here! It's great shelter. You can have the long space. I'll sleep in the shitter, if that's the way you're gonna be."

"No, no," said Jerry, laughing. "I'll tell you what. Let's put the tent up under that rock overhang, just outside. My bag's good, yer always in a scramble with that tissue paper bag you got. You sleep in here, in the shitter."

Jerry opened up the door again. He closed it just as quickly. "On second thought, damn it's cold! Tell you what. You take this, I'll take the tent at the overhang. If I get cold, I'll come in here, in the shitter!"

"In the shitter," I repeated. "Yo, suck ice, in the shitter! I'm likin' it already."

Jerry stepped outside. He immediately reversed himself and tried to get back inside just as I tried to get out. We thudded into each other—and into the door—at the same time.

"Oh, pardon me," I said, butler-like.

"That's okay," said Jerry. "By the way, it's freezing out there. How about you and I going out for dinner? In the shitter!"

"You mean, *this* shitter?"

"Yeah," he said. "Dinner in *this* shitter. It's shelter!"

"Now yer talkin'," I replied. "Dinner in this shitter, at five on the stool!"

"Lid down?"

"Lid down, promise! Let's unload; it's getting late and cold. I mean, *really* cold."

We made our way down the steps and toward our packs. Jerry was muttering in the dark. "Damn flashlight, dinner at five, oh man."

We got the tent set up under the rock overhang, and instead of using double ground covers, we'd both use our own, folded over. We covered and rocked down our packs and ponchos. Then, with our food bags in tow and our eating gear—cups, knives, and frying pans—plus our night clothes, we tromped back to the toilet.

Once inside, we proceeded to get into our thermal long johns, heavier socks, caps, and balaclavas. With our flashlight beams darting about like lasers, we must've looked like elves busy at Christmas time.

"Damn, Jer, you're hoggin' the place."

"Haven't you got room in yer own corner?" he countered.

"Yep! Nope!"

We managed to get dressed into our warm clothes, and finally took up our eating positions. With flashlight beams streaking left and right inside the small shelter, we began the ritual that we looked forward to each day: the last meal.

The pumped-up Peak-1 stove—Old Faithful—ignited on the first attempt. Immediately our home away from home was just that.

We cupped our hands and fingers around the base of the tiny stove for warmth. Slowly and gradually, the air temperature rose ever so slightly; it was those few degrees that made all the difference in the world as the dollhouse-like structure took on the ambiance of a wilderness cabin.

Using our frying pans and cups, we scooped up snow from outside the doorway and melted the shavings into our version of Black Mountain Whiskey.

Our appetites soared as we ate fried potatoes and onions, a half of bell pepper each, and a small tin of chicken split between us. We ate in savage-like silence, ending the meal by indulging in our final treat: cups of hot Jell-O®!

It was finished too soon. Oh, how we wanted to keep the stove going, but off it had to go. It was back to flashlights and cold.

We hung the food bags from a nail above the toilet stool; no big deal, as we only had four more planned meals. The bags—

actually, one inside the other—were light. If a bear, or other critter, large or small, was crazy enough to be out in this kind of weather, they could have our food, for a price! It would be a battle!

Jerry headed for the tent. It was actually as good a shelter as the toilet, except for the fact that he would be closer to the ground where the cold comes from. But, there was a heavy layer of duff underneath—pine needles, and such. He'd be okay.

Inside the cabin, I fluffed out my sleeping bag, laid out my pad and my doubled-over space blanket. I kept my heaviest socks on, along with my thermals—tops and bottom—and my cap and balaclava. My jacket would be my pillow. What few clothes I had left over would go into my sleeping bag with me, except for my work socks, which I hung next to the food bags. My flashlight and knife lay on the toilet lid.

I stretched out as best I could, half-way wrapping myself around the metal toilet base. Yes, it was a decent shelter. It got me off the cold ground, a roof over my head, and Jerry had the tent all to himself, a luxury when you consider the actual size of two-man tents.

As I began to succumb to the efforts of the day, my thoughts again drifted back to November of 1963, when my buddy and I were riding cross-country, on bicycle, through parts of Utah and Arizona. One late and freezing night, we literally crammed ourselves—and our bikes—into a Chevron® gas station restroom. It was Mt. Carmel Junction, Utah. My buddy and I were so hungry and cold that we tried to steal an apple pie that had been set out to cool at the back of a screened porch. I had actually started to cut the screen, when a blast went off from inside the house. We thought it was a shotgun, but we didn't stick around to ask questions. We ran toward a creek out back, and actually stumbled into the icy water. We hid, half frozen, until we thought it was safe enough to come out and to move!

The 6,000 foot elevation Utah night was freezing, and, by chance, a Chevron station was just down the way from where we were. It had an unlocked restroom. That's where we spent the night, bikes and all!

We'd put the bikes on end, and my buddy and I slept, sitting up, wrapped in our Korean War vintage sleeping bags. We left early the next morning; we were okay, but no apple pie.

We'd also spent the night in a drunk tank, as 'sleepers,' in Wilcox, Arizona. Then, there was the jail in St. George, Utah—the jail since demolished—and the rescue mission in El Paso, Texas, like the hold of a pirate ship it was!

And finally...the shitter!

For some strange reason, I thought back to Nightmare Canyon, when Jerry had caught a huge, hairy tarantula in his shirt! He brought it back to show me, the damned thing jumped out and tried to attack, or at least that's what it looked like to me.

"Are we having fun, yet?" Jerry had said.

I remember thinking, *here we are trapped in some godforsaken canyon, miles from nowhere, and Jerry is out huntin' for bugs! I'll be damned!*

I was thankful for Jerry and myself that night. We had survived thus far:

Yes siree-bob, this is livin'.

By the way, use of the toilet was by appointment only.

CHAPTER 13

DAY 13

Outpost Meadow

It was the crunch of footsteps that woke me up.

Still half asleep and with my head buried deep inside the hood of my sleeping bag, I rolled to the right and bumped into the hard toilet base. I could sense the cold surface through the fabric of my bag.

"Yo, Jerry!" I piped. "That you?"

"Yo, partner!" came the reply. "You bring ice skates?"

I quickly unzipped my bag and poked my head out of the warmth. Even from inside the structure, I could feel—and see—that it was dull outside, a subdued sunlight hung in the air: *canopy lighting*, I thought. *Sweet light!* The kind you get just before the actual debut of daybreak—or an overcast sky? I could rationalize. I could hope.

"What's the sky like?" I asked, loud enough for Jerry to hear me from inside. I was already gauging the cold from the way my trousers felt as I hurriedly pulled them on.

"Can't tell for sure," he continued. "Like fog out here, low ceiling."

I retrieved my socks from the homemade clothesline above. For some strange reason, I thought maybe, just maybe, those socks might be warm, like maybe they'd been blessed by warm air. But no! Not the case. As I struggled with the half-frozen socks, my enthusiasm dipped considerably about the prospects of the temperature outside.

Exiting the toilet house, however, didn't seem any worse than staying inside; it didn't feel that bad. That was always the case as I mentally tried to warm myself to the degree my brain was hoping for.

Jerry wasn't kidding. We found ourselves in a low cloud, as if someone had attached us to the end of a long pole and then stuck us up in the air to test the weather.

"Fog's makin' it halfway warm," I mumbled, as I carefully made my way down the heavily iced stairway, while trying to sound as rational as possible without seeming like a total jerk with such a declaration.

"Yeah, fifteen degrees warm," said Jerry.

"That's what you got?" I nodded toward the tent, where I could see Jerry's tiny thermometer hanging outside at the edge of the door flap. "Land-a-Goshen," I said. "Shorts weather!"

We both chuckled and pushed our hands deeper into our pockets.

"Shit, where's my gloves?" I mumbled, as we wandered off in opposite directions to check the area. We hadn't done so the night before. As we briefly separated, we weren't exploring with any particular direction or pattern in mind, but just kind of wandering, aimlessly, I guess. Really—when you get right down to it—we were just trying to get our blood moving, to fully wake up, we were trying to start our day.

"Yo, Jer, look over here!" I shouted.

I had moved to a clearing a short distance from the toilet. The cloud cover was higher at that point, and I could see part of The Wall up ahead. I could only see the base, since the top ridge was still heavily shrouded.

Jerry scurried over.

"It snowed pretty good last night," I said with a tinge of excitement. "Look at all that white!"

"Damn right it did," replied Jerry. "Us being in the trees here held it back some, but gawd-a-mighty, look at that wall!"

With fifteen degrees showing, we hadn't expected anything less. From the tiny subcreek and miniature fall that ran through our camp area, to The Wall ahead, to the traces of frozen snow on the ground where we stood, everything was either frozen, or white, or both.

Even the front half of Jerry's tent—the portion pointing away from the rock overhang—was drifted with a fine mist. The white crystals diminished, as they blended toward the opposite rock end.

As our bodies' inbuilt thermostats gradually readjusted themselves—going from the confines of warm sleeping bags to the outside—Jerry and I finally felt it, the *real* cold!

My earlier hope of warmth and sunshine slowly faded into the drabness around us, as we carefully walked back up the frozen steps of the toilet.

Once again, our reliable Peak-1 stove was fired into action. Our fingertips slowly regained some semblance of feeling as we fried up the contents of a can of Spam along with almonds and chopped apple. As our bellies and minds regained a sense of normalcy, our conversation contained the excitement of getting closer to a beginning—or an end—of an ordeal, and the disappointment of possibly calling it quits and going back down.

Those options were nothing new, as we had both realized from the beginning that we would—and could—only do so much. Therefore, our plans really hadn't been challenged, they would remain the same: go as far as we could, check it out, and go from there.

Shoving my gear to the corner of the toilet structure, we both stood to eat, while doing the Korean Stomp, a term born of the Korean War, though no less applicable to any cold weather situation. It consisted of standing and rocking from one leg to the other, bumping against the opposite foot as one did so. It helped with circulation in the feet and helped prevent frostbite. It is similar to what push-ups would do for the upper body.

With the stove raised up to the closed toilet lid, we alternated our frying pans, on and off the stove, to warm and rewarm the Spam, almonds and apple. At the same time, we methodically rocked out to the Korean Stomp and wondered how far we'd get that day—a far cry from 110 degree Badwater, a hundred miles away.

Packing helped warm us up, and as we left our home away from home, we knew we were probably leaving behind our last significant shelter. We also realized, with mixed emotion, that The Wall might be as far as we were going.

I watched Jerry as he snubbed up the last of his pack straps, goggles swung carelessly around his neck. His old brown jacket was tattered and duct-taped together, his baggy trousers had bog mud still showing in parts. His Hi-Tec boots were still half wet and half dry, and way off the original color. His gloves and watch cap, and whatever he had stuffed around his neck, allowed only a glimpse of his face, but I could see a mixture of beard, concern, and cold! You can always see cold in a man's face, and it was there!

His chapped lips and squinted eyes added to the weathered façade of determination, and the days of restless sun had produced a desert-like tan that made one consider the debt of such an ordeal, and suddenly, it all came in as a half-blurred perspective.

He had aged! But it looked good. Jerry looked the way a man should look, and I was proud. Proud of both of us.

I recalled when we started the journey and how fresh everything was. If anyone could've seen us then—and then, through time-lapse, fast forward to our present morning—they would have seen the price we had paid. And I, seeing it from day-to-day, could still see it and feel it! I didn't need a mirror, I could imagine what I looked like. By looking at Jerry, I knew, I knew.

For a split second, I was stunned by it all. Why the abruptness? I couldn't really answer that, except for the fact that I'd probably been in a state of denial all along. But for those few, brief moments, I simply stopped; I shut down. I saw us as we really were.

As I watched Jerry, I saw a part of myself. I saw it all, I *felt* it all!

It was good to move. Our packs felt snug and secure, as if they had been transformed into huge, lightweight parkas. After all, the clothing that had been carried *inside* our packs was now *outside*—on our bodies. It was simply a matter of redistribution.

Our food supply was next to nothing. *Is there a difference between having it in our bellies, or in our packs?*

Even our water supply was lighter. We weren't carrying two quarts each on top of everything else.

Besides the weight issue, Jerry and I knew that our packs also served as a protective covering, a buffer, so to speak, like the bumper on a truck or a car if we were to take a fall or hit.

Unlike mountain summer, there was the added bonus of not having to hang our food away from bears and other scavengers: no counters, hi-ties, pop-ups, or swing lines.

In other words, we respected and appreciated our packs as if they were wives, we knew something about them, we belonged to them, and they to us.

So, as we struggled that morning with the increased gain in mountain altitude, the comparable workload increased also, but, in our case, we had lightened the overall weight of our packs in sort of a man-wife trade off. We had to get along, our packs and us, and we kept moving up.

As for Jerry and I, we felt we could move and maneuver as good as anything up on the mountain that day. And with our physical beings in top shape—plus being considerably lighter, ourselves, in actual body weight—our mind-set suddenly kicked into a positive high gear. With that going full speed, it would literally take a mountain—a *big* mountain—to stop us!

So, regardless of the weather and the temperamental nature of our chill-touched brains, we could still draw from the positive. We were alive and well. What more could we have asked for?

This was a replay of the bogs, but in reverse. On the bogs, we sought relief from the ungodly heat. At Whitney, we would seek relief from the bitter cold. Like on the bogs, when the sun finally broke through, it too, all of a sudden, shined upon us at Whitney! Not to cook us, but to warm our spirits and to show us the way.

"Jerry! Look, look, look over there!" I shouted. "Sunshine! It's coming through!"

Jerry jumped onto a large boulder. He was shielding the sun from his eyes.

The sun had broken through at a point probably a mile ahead of us, toward The Wall, where the ceiling was evidently weakest. The resultant sunspot, outlined on the ground, grew bigger and bigger. It moved toward us, or rather, it grew big enough to engulf us, as we proceeded forward, and up.

"Gawd dang!" one of us shouted.

"Yah-hoooo!"

As we yipped and shouted, we threw a snowball or two at each other.

"Are we havin' fun yet?"

"Yo! Suck ice!"

Excitedly, we drew up together to watch the gigantic sunspot.

"Man, look at those clouds scatter, there's blue up there!"

"Look, look at the ridge. It's opening up!"

"Damn, Sam! Look at that, will ya!"

The phenomenon of the warming was spectacular. The sun struck us; we were ecstatic! The clouds and fog raced over us like reckless climbers on a broken cliff, bouncing and scattering left to right, west to east. We watched in awe as other unfamiliar faces and figures rushed overhead.

Even though our breathing had become more labored the higher we went, our renewed enthusiasm and excitement spurred us on, and at a good pace. No, it wasn't warm by any stretch of the imagination. In fact, the air began to feel even *colder* as the protection of the cloud cover dissipated.

Then, just as suddenly as the sun appeared, the inevitable happened, the scourge of all living things.

Wind!

I practically yelled at Jerry as he trudged up. "Damn, it's messin' with us again!" Then I lamented in a quieter tone, "We dropped our guards, damned if we didn't. Jerry, I'll tell ya, the minute you think you got it whipped, it kicks your butt, after all these years."

"We don't need wind," said Jerry, threateningly. "Damned if we don't."

"Yeah," I said, almost remorsefully. "Feel it! *It is* coming up."

"Been better off with the clouds," said Jerry, catching his breath. "Sometimes a storm is better than the aftereffect."

"Oh well, we should've expected it. You know, low pressure moves over and out then it sucks in the wind." I kicked at the snow, then looked skyward. "Could've been worse," I continued, "could've had more storm, *plus* wind! Oh well, whatever the rules."

"What rules?" quipped Jerry, talking back over his shoulder. "We shoulda stayed in the toilet, watched TV…coulda looked down the shitter."

"Quit lookin' down the damn thing, man. That's your reflection." I watched my boot as it pressed a tread mark into the hard packed snow.

"Oh yeah," pondered Jerry. "Thought it looked familiar."

"How's that?" I asked.

"Oh nothing, just the shitter."

"You mean lookin' down it?"

"Yeah, reminds me of TV."

"You mean it's that bad?" I asked.

"Well, just sitting and staring, lots of wasted time."

"You mean you'd rather be here, staring at clouds and freezin' your ass off?"

"Sorta, wouldn't trade it. You know that."

We stopped, briefly, and began to move around, restlessly. The wind increased and the cold became more pronounced. Jerry continued, "You know what I mean? One extreme to the other. We know just as we stand here, that there's millions who'll never understand what it's like out here. Like I said, they're all watching TV; it's a symbol, a symbol of how far in reverse we've come. Know what I mean?"

Jerry stared at me. He looked serious, tired, glazed.

"Yeah man, I know what you mean. Ain't it grand out here? We havin' fun yet?"

We both laughed sedately. It was good to see a smile come across Jerry's face, a good sign.

"Hell, it's the altitude," I said, "We're skitzin' out! Let's get up this mountain before we freak all the way!"

We were both aware of the judgmental effects of altitude and how behavior can change, radically. We were aware that our judgment calls could be critical. Couple that with the cold and fatigue, and situations can become extreme, we both knew that.

The landscape became more and more lunar as the starkness and isolation of a granite world began to manifest itself. To a newcomer, and the inexperienced, such an unworldly place is intimidating, part of the planet that *must* be respected and dealt with, but *only* by the initiated. Even then, the odds of survival can be drawn to a very thin line.

The wind held its steady push, though it was tolerable as far as high mountains go—what would we expect at 12,000 feet in late October? It was a rob-Peter-to-pay-Paul-situation at that point. We were fully clothed, and working upgrade, and generating body heat. In other words, we were at a moderate comfort level, as long as we kept moving. If we stopped, we'd feel it! So, we kept moving. Simple!

As we continued, Jerry began to mumble about pizza, and double and triple burgers, and corn-on-the-cob with tons of melted butter. I responded in kind, though my preference was fried chicken and a two-tier chocolate cake with frosting. Once again—though ever so briefly—I thought I caught the drift of perfume, a fragrance! And there was a wisp of blondish hair.

Jerry began cleaning his goggles with one of his gloves, and how right-on that gesture would symbolize the whole scheme of things as we moved up higher, as the wind began to intensify with more moderate whips and gusts, it somehow began to remind me of a swarm of winter bees seeking a direction.

And The Wall was dead ahead, we were at Trail Camp.

We had a second surprise encounter; we met two men on their way down. Their report on what we would find ahead was the same as what we received the day before. They knew of no way we could get through the switchbacks without proper equipment. It was all ice, and all they had in the way of gear were ice axes! They decided it wasn't worth risking their lives, so they had turned around. They were emphatic about the danger.

Jerry and I listened and studied the men. They, too, had heard about our trekking from Death Valley, but we didn't want to talk about us. No! It was the switchbacks we wanted to hear about.

Their report was somewhat meaningless since Jerry and I could finally see for ourselves. The switchbacks were dead ahead, vertically! At least it was the right direction, since whatever trail was supposedly there was under all that white and gleam that lay directly ahead of us by five hundred yards. That's where the pipe handholds would be; that would be the start of the switchbacks!

The two men wanted to talk about a lot of things. In fact, they rambled on to such an extent that it became evident that they were inexperienced and were very glad to see someone else up there. They had spent a rough night in the cold and snow, and they were elated that they had survived it all.

It's a confidence kind of thing that one experiences when completing a difficult mission or similar endeavor, or when one has overcome extreme odds to come away a winner. It can make one excited and talkative!

I told the new men about two others who had died there, at Trail Camp, some years back when that area had been struck by the hurricane, Norman. And how two others had died at Lamarck Col—a col is a small dip—during the same storm, and how my former wife and I had survived the onslaught in a tube tent, no less, at the base of Colby Pass.

The ones who had died were ill-prepared for backcountry work, and didn't realize—or hadn't learned, or been taught—that weather, at altitude, could be disastrous!

As Jerry and I continued our exchange with the new men, we, too, were cognizant of the weather. And like nervous cats—looking and listening at the same time—it was obvious that our attention was directed toward The Wall. We were anxious!

The men finally moved on and Jerry and I continued our march forward—and up.

The wind increased and there were fewer clouds. The early afternoon sun was heading toward the top ridge and it would soon arc over to the other side. We'd be left in deep, cold shadow.

We continued to trudge along in silence; both of us were deep in thought as to what, and how, our final reaction would be as we neared the possible end of our journey. It was coming too soon. After all those days, we couldn't just walk up and touch the stone and say, "Well, that's it!"

How could it be? We hadn't planned on such an ending. There would be no drama at that point, no expectation, no finale! It simply *could not* end in such a way. No! It couldn't be! Why was the mountain trying to steal it away from us?

Finally, finally, it was directly before us: The Wall!

We simply walked to the end of the trail—there it was. It was exactly like it looked from a distance and from the reports we had received: a massive stone wall of white!

Metal poles jutted upward from out of the ice. There was a piece of six-strand cable between the first two standards, but from that point on, there was not much else. A few metal poles that grew shorter and shorter, or rather, deeper and deeper into the white frosting. After that, there was nothing but ice!

"Good gawd," exclaimed Jerry, in total awe. "Those guys were right. It's solid!"

"Yeah," I said, thoughtfully. "Yeah, it's solid! This baby's here for the winter."

We squinted as we surveyed the huge slab, from bottom to top, where the lingering, sun-reflected snow held its position. We stared in wonder as the ice-cooled wind swept down from the top of the ridge.

"We better take lunch," I said, not really feeling hungry, but wanting to do something—anything—other than just standing there like a frozen dummy.

We ate, though it wasn't leisurely. We walked in small circles as we munched on an apple, six prunes a piece, and a carrot split between us. There wasn't much room between ice and rock.

We were nervous; we felt caged in! We didn't want to stop moving, and it was getting colder.

Suddenly, "Lee, look! Two of 'em!"

I snapped my head up to where Jerry was pointing. "What? Where?"

I saw two dark blotches, south and west of us, on the ice, maybe one thousand yards up.

"Damn, climbers!" Jerry yelped. "Couple of 'em comin' down! Maybe it's those UK guys we heard about."

"Holy shit!" I clamored, tripping over a large rock as I tried to get into position next to Jerry. "Are you sure? Your eyes are better than mine! Whadda ya see? Whadda ya see!"

I tried to shield the brilliant sun from my eyes as I scanned above; Jerry was digging for his binos.

"Hold it! Hold it!" he said excitedly, as he situated himself against a chunk of ice-covered rock. "I got 'em, see 'em. Yeah, hell, there's two of 'em, comin' down."

"Come on!" I yelped. "Let's meet 'em, they must have a route!" I almost choked on my carrot.

"Damn," said Jerry, pulling the glasses slowly away from his face. "Just when it's darkest, it gets brighter, it's starting to shine! Let's roll!"

And we did!

Jerry and I began working our way along and over the rocks at the edge of the ice. It was like a bluff that outlined the lower shelf of the huge white wall. We would attempt to intercept the two climbers as they worked their way down.

It seemed as though the climbers saw us, too, as they began to move toward our line of direction.

Working in sidestep, the two figures slowly and methodically zigzagged across the steep face. They were working toward us on a diagonal line. In essence, they were cutting their own switchback, a logical maneuver when you must go up or down a steep pitch—snow or not.

Jerry and I moved at about the same rate, as best we could without crampons, over a combination of ice and rock, going straight across, left to right. We had to eventually work slightly below the ice line in order to maintain a secure footing. All in all, our travel was sufficient. We'd be able to strike a common point to meet up with the two climbers.

The figures were men. They were from Great Britain, and when they spoke, their strong British accents pretty well substantiated that fact. We shook hands and joked about the White Cliffs of Dover, while at the same time, throwing imaginary glances toward and above us all, toward The Wall.

It's difficult to explain, but for a brief segment of time, there was a mutual feeling of comradeship—a camaraderie, if you will—that was totally different from the other brief meetings with the others earlier on.

The Brit climbers looked the part of a high-tech, rock generation, young and careless, but somewhat experienced; it seemed to show, there was a look, or demeanor, about them.

Jerry and I, on the other hand, were the oldest. We portrayed that ambiance of a tattered and worn generation, but tougher in a more sustained way, and wise to the ways of the world by virtue of the fact that we'd simply been around just a little longer than they had.

The climbers had been out for a weekend. Jerry and I, well, that's an old story, literally!

Therefore, a mutual respect. Like coming in from patrol, the fatigued meeting the fresh.

The formalities were over as quickly as we had met. The main point for Jerry and me was: how, when, where, and so on. How far did you get? What were the conditions, and the like?

And the sun finally dropped behind the ridge.

Very briefly, the climbers said that they had gotten to the 13,000 foot, lower summit, but no information about beyond.

Jerry and I were ecstatic! If *they* had gotten that far, then so could *we*, plus more, all the way!

We thanked the two climbers for their information and watched as they continued their way downward, the same route that Jerry and I just struggled over.

We huddled quickly.

"My gawd! We have a crampon line to follow!" My thoughts were in high gear, and the sudden glance I got from Jerry indicated he was thinking the same thing.

It would be anybody's guess, however, as to what it would be like from that point on—less than two miles to the very top!

No matter how experienced those guys seemed to be, we—Jerry and I—had to keep in mind that we were taking in secondhand information. We would soon see, and understand, that all that glitters was not necessarily gold.

We would almost bet our lives on that.

A crucial judgment call had to be made, as Jerry and I were up against a critical turning point, it was late in the day, my thoughts went into high gear:

"Probably three in the afternoon; might make the 13,000 foot lower summit by five, roughly a mile-and-a-half from there to the final top 14,490-plus feet.

Sun had just dipped behind the main ridge, which put us into deep shadow and a rapidly dropping temperature. It had been fifteen degrees at our last shelter at nine that morning; it had risen to twenty-two degrees by one that afternoon, but plummeted to eleven degrees in a matter of fifteen minutes as the sun disappeared over the ridge.

In regard to wind, it was steady, but not critical at that point, since Jerry and I were physically up against the leeward side of The Wall, and the wind was actually rushing over us, west to east. We were well aware of that blow-by phenomenon—less wind at the actual base—knowing full well that it could be blowing at gale force at, and over, the top of the ridge, which is usually the case for high mountain passes and cols.

What to do? Roll the dice!

Bet that the wind would settle by dusk or hold for the night and start up again come morning. Or will it double in intensity and blow all through the night and be gone by morning?

Another roll of the dice. Retreat to a lower level elevation bivouac, freeze our asses off, and start anew come morning, but be another day behind, and chance more storm.

We were anxious. We saw the possibility of moving ahead. After all, we had tracks to follow! We also knew of a flat, walled-in shelter at the 13,000 foot level where we could've probably gotten a tent up. We also knew about the stone hut shelter at the very summit of Whitney, but we knew nothing of the conditions from the 13,000 foot level up, from that point on. The big question, of course: did we have sufficient gear to hold out in sub-zero conditions?

Colder by the minute, we had to do something, pronto! Regardless, it was unanimous. We'd go for it!"

Probably the most influential factor was the sun disappearing behind the ridge. The ensuing bitter cold was dangerous. We could freeze to death under such circumstances. We had no more time to wait and ponder. No more long cold nights wondering about The Wall. We were there! We'd shoot for it and get it over with!

With chapped and freezing hands and split fingertips, we struggled with our cold-steeled crampons, strapping them tightly to each boot underside, making sure that the ankle straps were especially tight. Nothing would be more frustrating—or dangerous—than having a crampon come loose in the middle of a tough pitch. You'd get double and triple jeopardy: cold hands—you can't work straps with gloves on—ice and snow jammed between metal and boot, and being in a place where crampon use would be critical. In our particular case, there would be a fourth factor: Jerry had ball crampons only—a single metal cleat that would fit over the ball of the foot or boot. My opinion? Outlaw them! Full boot only, the only *safe* way to go!

Onto our ice axes, we had attached lanyards—short pieces of rope affixed to the ax itself. This was in case you'd lose your grip and wind up watching that piece of lightweight metal sail off into the wild white yonder. In other words, it was mandatory that you have a safety lanyard attached to the ice ax in case it was accidentally dropped.

With crampons attached, I gingerly trod across the rough scree and crunched onto the snow-ice. Jerry followed. It felt good to have the spikes on, and to feel the secure footing from underneath. We soon appreciated the fact that if all conditions were favorable, we could skim our way across a lot of rough country just *because* of the snow cover. For the first hour, that's exactly how it went, and, thus, we generated a positive rationale in *favor* of the snow. The downside, of course, was the associated cold and wet, and the fact that snow never seems to manifest itself during the warmer months—like summer! No, of course not! Snow means winter, winter means cold!

The positive aspect of mushing across a snowfield, that in turn, smoothed over all the rough terrain below, finally gave way to a negative payback: the pitch became steeper!

We continued in a switchback pattern, following the crampon lead of the last two climbers. But as the pitch became more severe and jagged rocks began to appear out of the snow and ice, like giant dorsal fins, it became evident that the previous climbers had been indecisive. Their tracks indicated so; they went in circles and we could see where they'd probed with their axes. Then, there'd be a straight shot, and it would ease up, then they'd stopped again as if to plan their next move.

We came to a branching out, or a split-off, and their up route intermeshed with their down tracks. Then Jerry and I became confused as to whether they moved up, or down.

Finally, it leveled off again, and the climbers' ice ax trail became comfortable: drag, punch; drag, punch; drag, punch! In other words, when travel was relatively level, or easy, the climbers had eased their stride, to a drag-and-punch. By a line, or mark in the crusty snow surface, we could see where they had dragged the tip ends of their ice axes across the snow as they took one step forward, then punching in the ax, for support, as they brought up the other foot. If Jerry and I had been wolves, we would've recognized, even more so, the climbers' confusion and indecision at times, as the pitch became steeper and rougher. Wolves can recognize a limp by the track; Jerry and I could *see* the confusion.

I held the lead at roughly thirty feet ahead of Jerry, just enough distance to take a rope, if need be, from either me to him, or from him to me.

The side of The Wall became even steeper, our breathing more labored, and our rest intervals more frequent.

The wind was practically dead still, but as I glanced upward, toward the crest, above, it seemed as though I could see wisps of cloud, or wild snow, being blown over the top.

Damn, I thought, *it's blowing like crazy on top, but maybe not, maybe my eyes are blurred, maybe it's my brain, hope it's not blowing, hope not.*

The deep shade, or shadow, that we'd been thrust into became more subtle, more dense, and there was a hue, or a filmy haze that seemed to be forming. It seemed to be purple and I briefly rubbed my eyes with the back of my glove, it must've been the white hue of snow reflecting back to the waning, dark blue of sky that, in turn, emitted a sort of borealis, the purple, and it was becoming even more so.

"Yo, Jerry!" I shouted. I suddenly wanted to hear myself, like whistling in the dark when one becomes afraid. "You okay?"

"Yo, okay," he shouted back. Even with gloves on, my fingertips were beginning to tingle as if tiny electrically ionized impulses were being sent from somewhere out of space.

I looked back once again, toward Jerry, and suddenly began to realize that we were on a cold-hell, no-return mission. We were going forward no matter what.

Get used to it, I thought. *Accept it.*

Damn it, I have, leave me alone. I was arguing with myself, damned if I wasn't.

There we were, in the middle of a vast, white, no-man's land, and I flashed back to the bogs and their 110-degree heat. It, too, was vast and white and lonely, then it was Nightmare Canyon, then it was Rainbow Canyon. I didn't want that kind of isolation again; I didn't want that kind of steepness again, but there we were on a sheet of white that was transfixed in a haze of light purple. Kool-Aid® it was, punch: too sweet to drink, maybe bitter, maybe bitter-sweet. Hell with it! And it all became slowly, and strangely inconsequential: which way was up or down anymore? It was like being churned and tumbled about in a giant, slow-motion sea wave.

But sure enough, there we were, on The Wall!

Again, I looked up ahead, and then back to Jerry, and the cold was cold. Real cold!

Ironically, I felt warm, except for my hands. The warmth came from our work. How cold would it get if we were to stop? Or had to stop? We couldn't work forever.

We kept moving.

We kept to the previous climbers' tracks which zigzagged across the face of The Wall, but to the left, or south, of the actual trail route. That meant that the 13,000 foot level we were shooting for, would be to our right, or to the north, of our location. That was okay; it seemed like we were moving in the right direction.

But up ahead, Hell! Wait a minute. Something wasn't right. A drop off! A *big* drop off! A steep cut, *an ice chute!*

"Yo, Jer, better move up!"

I tromped a small circle in the snow for a standing place. We needed a break. We *both* had to see the cut up ahead.

Jerry pulled up.

"How's those cramps doing?" I asked. "They gonna be okay? I don't know why they even make those damned things, should have full boot." I caught my breath, "Full crampons, you gonna be okay?"

"Yeah." Jerry took a big breath also. He was blowing steam, and I watched my own breath in front of my face as we spoke back-and-forth. We were working hard; it made for good steam.

"Yo, steam!" I joked.

"Suck ice," said Jerry, good naturedly. "Suck big chunks of ice, ugh! Me like ice, me like The Wall, me heap big husky!" Jerry laughed, so did I. It felt good.

I purposely held my breath, and then let out a long draw of steam.

Suddenly, a wisp of wind caught us off guard.

"Shit!" one of us said. "That motha's cold!"

"That it is, my man, that it is."

We started doing the Korean Stomp within our little circle of snow and ice, and we both stared at the cut-away chute off to our right. It was massive, it was steep, it was all ice as far down as one could see, maybe one thousand feet. We really didn't know for sure how far down it was, but it was a very long way.

And who measures such things? Do men hang down, by rope, with measuring devices? Do they rappel like acrobatic flies who then flit back and forth, like veteran players on a checker board? Are they like the men who scaled the cliffs above Hoover Dam, breaking away all the loose debris prior to actual construction? And as told even today, were men re*ally* buried beneath all that concrete, below that fabled dam?

I snapped back to the actual moment, to that actual point on The Wall where Jerry and I stood. Were men possibly buried below *us*, in all that ice and rock?

It was akin to looking over the face of a huge dam; that's what that cut-away looked like—a frozen water chute. Yeah, it did look like what you'd see at Hoover Dam: slick, concrete-slabbed chutes coming off the sides like some kind of overflow channel. I could imagine a huge rooster tail of water shooting out, and beyond, I shuttered to think about being caught and swept away.

In our own thoughts, that's what it was all about. That's what ice chutes do, that's what minds do.

"My gawd," I suddenly whispered in disbelief. "We're on the *wrong side*! But look! Look, Jer!" I raised my voice in renewed excitement. "Look! It's the summit, right above us! Isn't that the 13,000?"

I grabbed Jerry's arm and pointed to a small col that was above us, along the ridge, and to our right, maybe a couple hundred yards distant.

"You might be right," said Jerry, looking beleaguered, and squinting upward toward that direction.

He was the cagey Field Marshal Rommel once again, but this time he was fatigued, weary. He had faced his foe and had been at it for a while, hood up, balaclava wrapped around his neck, goggles hanging loose and lopsided with straps twisting in and out and around his jacket collar and scarf-like balaclava. He blew steam when he talked, but there was enthusiasm; he was tougher than ever.

"We're closer than we thought," he continued, "but you're right, we're on the wrong side of the chute! All the switchbacks are on the other side. No wonder they built the trail over there."

"It looks worse over there," I countered. "The pitch, damned steep!"

"We've got to trail this thing out," said Jerry, looking up ahead and toward the top of the ice chute. "Where'd those guys go, anyway?"

"Let's move it up, keep following their tracks, see where they went." I was stomping snow, trying to hold the warmth that we'd generated within our bodies.

But it was difficult. The snow was freezing harder, and our cramponed boots and ankles would twist and turn as we continued to track the iced-up trail left by the other climbers.

The sky continued to turn darker, and the insidious purple hue was still mysteriously evident. The minute we stopped, or slowed down, the cold knifed in like frozen blades and the wind began to gust; it was stronger!

"We *must* be near the summit!" I shouted back. "The wind, picking up! We're starting to catch the blow-by!"

As we moved further up, we could no longer see the perimeter that clearly outlined our newest location alongside the southeast flank of the chasm. As we neared the top lip of the ice chute, the steepness put us even closer to The Wall, which definitely closed off our upward view.

It was like climbing up the side of a frozen milk pitcher, and how you could suddenly be thrust up, under the top lip that rimmed the edge, that's what it was like, like a parapet.

And we were nearing that parapet! The parapet was a snow-iced ridge that would lip the ridgeline during the winter. Snow and ice would freeze out in a solid, overhand formation, all caused by heavier winds that would sculpt from the backside. What would the 13,000 foot lower level be like, and could we even get to it?

But that was okay. The British climbers had said they'd gotten that far!

Jerry and I kept moving up, slowly, and the sky continued to draw darkness, and the wind continued to become gustier. Then, as Jerry pulled up, briefly, I glanced at his thermometer: *seven-degrees!*

I flashed back to Korea. Men, there too, walked in small circles, and they looked ahead, and up. There were ridges there, too, frozen ridges, and I thought about the 40,000 to 50,000 men who perished in that short, brutal—but forgotten—war and how as many lives were lost in three years as were lost in the nine years of Vietnam.

It was a mountainous war fought in a climate that ranged from monsoons—with mud slides that would make Malibu slides pale by comparison—to bitter cold that froze the liquid in canteen cups. Subzero temperatures froze up our M-1's and cracked mortar barrels. It made men dig underground, like moles, in search of warmth: bunkers and caves. It was damp and wet, feet were rotten and fingers, toes, ear lobes, and noses were frostbitten, not excluding my own fingers.

I turned back to Jerry. "Yo, we havin' fun yet?"

He gave a thumbs up.

"Just think. Our very own ridge!" I chimed.

I turned back again. Jerry was clapping his gloved hands together, and sort of running in place. His legs were cold and stiff.

"Yo, partner," I shouted. "Let's do it! Let's find the way!"

"Let's do it!" he repeated. "Let's kick the crap outta this mountain!"

We moved up. The snow became deeper, but still crusty. It was like trudging across a massive Sno-Cone®, and each step became progressively tougher.

We began to stick, and each movement had to be carefully justified. We didn't want our crampons to become frozen in, or stuck, and we had to be careful about spiking ourselves as each step became more and more unpredictable.

We moved deliberately, and there were places that suddenly became vertical, right before us! We were actually able to touch The Wall, or so it seemed. Then we'd get a short run, and we'd work it, and the tracks we were trying to follow became more and more erratic.

We reached a short ledge. The previous climbers' tracks zigzagged all over the place, and all around. They'd probed with their axes and kicked-in with their crampons but where did they go? Where'd they go from there?

I raised my hand in a halt signal. We stopped. I slowly turned back to Jerry. "I don't see where they went," I said, almost zombie-like. "I don't see where they went from here!"

I had to say it twice; I had to hear my voice.

Suddenly, I felt as if someone had just slammed a door—a giant, white, steel door! And it closed right in front of us! A second door slammed from behind.

I swung around; it came from the left, then the right. I turned quickly in the other direction, I wanted to scream out, "No! No! This can't be! We're locked off, trapped!" My thoughts went wild for just a split second.

Be cool, yeah, man, be cool! I listened to my own labored breathing. My head had to clear; my heart had to slow down. "Close to thirteen thousand feet, maybe five degrees by now." I turned back to Jerry. He knew, he knew.

"Damn them!" I yelled. "Damn those Brits!" I drove the blade of my ice ax into the snow.

"Can you see, Jerry?" I shouted. "Can you see what those bastards did?" I slammed my ax down again.

I bent over and rested on one leg. *Be cool, man, be cool, settle down, don't waste energy, control, control, think! Be cool!*

I turned back to Jerry again. He was moving up.

"Is it what I think?" he muttered.

"Yeah, you got it. *This is as far they got*! Those airheads lied! And here we are, where they bailed; they quit and went back down. This is as far as they got! They never got to the thirteen thousand. Look there." I pointed. "That's where they turned."

"No wonder their tracks look so screwy," said Jerry. "Maybe they thought this was the 13,000 foot level?"

"Bullshit!" I blurted. "It just got too wild."

Jerry and I didn't look at each other. We knew the situation. In seconds, we shifted gears and re-evaluated.

"*We're* not going back," said Jerry, sternly.

"You got that right," I replied. "Too close, too close to the top!"

Jerry took a couple steps backward; I did the same. We both looked down.

"My, oh my," I said. "That's a mistake."

"What's that," blurted Jerry.

I chuckled, and sighed with relief. "Oh nothing, we shouldn't be lookin' down, that's all." I shook my head to clear it. "Look at it down there, one rugged S.O.B. Be worse going back down than going up."

"Yo," said Jerry.

"Yo, yo!" I mimicked. Snow flicked off our gloves as we high-fived.

"Ain't this grand?" I chirped, managing a smile.

"I feel like a frozen pickle," said Jerry.

"You look it," I said in return. "One frozen, green pickle!"

"Is that what color they are?"

We laughed.

"Oh well, whatever the rules," I clapped my hands together and looked ahead. "Got to move, my man, got to move."

It was back to business.

There were no guardians up there. Nobody to tell us right from wrong. No parents. No mama bears to cuff us if we made a false move. There would be no second-guessing or second judgment calls on our part. We wouldn't be able to pull the wool over anybody's eyes or sweet talk our way out of a jam. This wasn't school! No siree! We had to play it straight. No false moves from that point on.

The bogs had been intimidating, but we were fresh then, no altitude, clear heads. Today, we were blitzed! Altitude, cold, fatigue, we'd have to play it straight, no mistakes, we both knew that, it was tacit consent.

Evidently, the British climbers had gotten to where we were and turned back. They told us they'd reached the 13,000 foot level—but they hadn't—and we had taken their information as gospel. No, not all that glitters is gold!

It was too late in the day to try to circumvent a return route. We were too close to the 13,000 foot level, in addition to having to cross the ice chute that was smack-dab in front of us.

We decided to go all the way, even in the dark, even if conditions weren't totally in our favor. And, compared to where we were, it would be relatively flat up ahead, even with ice and snow, and probably wind!

Relying on the Brits' testimony had put the two of us in jeopardy. We had chosen to follow their tracks. Would we have pursued this last leg of our journey had we not met them? I didn't know. What I did know is that Jerry and I were specialists in cutting our own way, it was a quirk of fate in meeting the other two. With reckless abandon, we had taken their secondhand information, which ultimately put us in a tough situation.

We simply had to work it out.

We laid out thirty feet of rope. I took the lead after we agreed that only one of us would move at any one time, while the other would lock in. Then we'd change about. We repeated our instructions to each other, we had to comprehend! Communication was extremely important considering the element we were working in, as well as our fatigue and state of mind. Our brains had to be in gear and in sync!

We moved on. I cut to the left, then back to the right. I stopped, then Jerry moved. We watched each other. One would move, then lock in and watch the other, then trade off.

Working in such a manner, we did a slow and methodical zigzag, working around the top rocks of the ice chute. Our crampons struck rock and ice simultaneously, and, in certain areas, we could actually get handholds in the exposed roughened structure itself where it was too vertical to hold snow!

As we carefully traversed the top rock, dusk began to settle and it began to snow!

"Holy shit!" I blurted out. "Where's the stuff comin' from?" I strained to look up. It was clear overhead, yet it was snowing!

Suddenly, we could feel the wind gusts!

I took a few more steps. Easy, easy, easy. I locked in; Jerry moved up to the next higher level.

"Wadda ya got?" he shouted.

"It's snowing," I shouted back.

Jerry locked in, and I moved further out. I was practically on the top of the start of the ice-fall. I thumped my cramponed boot into the crust. I did it again. It didn't feel right. One more time. *Thump! Thud!*

Something was wrong. I thumped again. It felt *hollow*!

Oh shit! I thought. *Blow snow! That's why it's snowing! Jesus! God watch over us!* I was breathing heavily. I could feel ice crystals building on my balaclava, around my mouth and chin, and I was excited and scared at the same time. I suddenly didn't want to be where I was.

"Jer!" I yelled down. "Stay put, this is blow snow!" A heavier gust of wind rushed in, more snow fell, then another gust and more snow.

"Yo, Jer! Can you hear me okay?"

"Yeah," came his reply.

"Listen closely," I continued, as I brought my hand up to my mouth. I felt the ice, I could taste it. The wind blew harder, and each time it did, it snowed.

"Jer, the wind's going like hell across the top. It's blowing loose snow, all this crap across the chute is loose. That's why those guys turned back. It's damned loose! It could break away! Understand? Do you hear me okay?"

"Yeah, I hear you okay. Your insurance paid up?"

"What insurance? You're my insurance! Whaddya you going to do with *your* ten grand?" we were shouting to be heard above the howling wind!

"Open a Sno-Cone® stand in Death Valley!"

There was a long pause. I thought to myself, *Damn! Why didn't I think of that? He's onto something.*

"You okay?" Jerry yelled up.

"Yeah, yeah, yeah," My voice trailed off as I forced a smile. Then I chuckled to myself. *If I bow out here, I've at least got a smile on my face.*

I turned one more time toward Jerry and raised a fist. "Here's to the fourth of July, Death Valley! Yo, partner! I'm going across, lock in! Lock in!"

The wind increased, the sky turned a deeper purple, and the white world around us no longer seemed real. I could no longer feel the cold, I was numb!

The Big Push was on; total darkness would fall within an hour. The temperature was five degrees, with wind gusts of ten to fifteen miles per hour, the windchill factor was anybody's guess.

Disposition? Jerry and I were oblivious to anything else taking place in our lives. At that moment, our only concern was crossing the last hundred yards of ice chute. Nothing else mattered. We had to focus. Crossing the chute would be our rite of passage!

Our agreement, if one of us were to fall or be swept away, was that the other would not—under any circumstances—unduly risk his life for the other. If we both went together, then so be it!

Agreed, case closed!

I took another step. *Thud!* It felt like the whole top of the chute quivered! The snow's crust was weak and my boot punched in at a foot-and-a-half deep.

Prior to reaching the chute, the surface snow had been frozen pretty solid. On the chute, it was loose, blown snow from above. The chute's surface was fragile, fluffy blow snow!

Another step, another, thud! Thud! I turned back to Jerry. He was locked in, rope around his lower backside, in belay. He gave thumbs up.

The plan was to compact a trail across the top. Stomp and compress, make it as solid as possible. Besides compression, we'd chop in with our axes until we'd hit rock, establishing a handhold. That would be our safety: compress and establish a sound foothold, chop and establish handholds. Then—and only then—move to the next position.

I was first out, so that's what I was doing: stomp and compress, chop and hold! Move across, step-by-step, one foot at a time.

I came to the end of the thirty foot length of rope. I was ecstatic that I'd made it that far, and in my exuberance, I quickly and briefly flashed back to the time I had worked my way across a severely steep snowfield—180 feet; six, thirty-foot lengths of rope—using my metal camera tripod as an ax to dig in with, and there was water down below! Five other companions fed me the rope. Had I fallen, it was our theory that I would've swung like a pendulum back to the edge of the talus, and not to the water below.

The same should work for the ice chute. If either one fell, the second man would hold, and the one falling would arc back into the side of the chute. Then, with the attached rope, and with the help of the second man, he would climb back up.

It sounded simple.

"Yo, Jer! Tie on the other thirty feet!"

Jerry waved back and immediately went to work coupling up the second rope. We now had sixty feet.

I locked in and yelled for Jerry to move it up.

Jerry started his crossing and I slowly began to reel in the rope. He, too, stomped and hacked. I watched and thought out loud, "Come on, Jer, come on, man, easy does it."

He moved to the first mark. He locked in, then we reversed our moving positions. My turn—again. *Thud! Whack!*

The snow was deeper. It was like being on the bogs; everything trembled and quivered every time I stomped down or kicked in with my boot. I chopped away with the ice ax. I locked in and tightened up on the rope.

Jerry moved. I took up the slack in the rope and, even when he kicked in with his boot, I could feel vibration.

In angst, I shook my head. I questioned my sanity. "This *is* scary; damned scary!" I mumbled to myself. I looked down. Straight down! Mistake! "Don't look down, fool! Don't look!"

My turn again, several feet gained, I locked in.

It was Jerry's turn.

Whoosh!

The exact second I turned to glance toward our forward position, Jerry yelled out.

"Yeaaaa!!!"

I whipped back around just in time to see a large chunk of snow and ice giving way beneath him. With a mighty swing of his ice ax, Jerry drove the pick's end deep into the frozen wall that was to his left. It held! *He* held!

"Shit, Jerry!" I yelled. "Hang on! Damn it, hang on!" Instinctively, I jerked hard on the rope and reared back onto it, in belay. Rock, snow, ice, and dark-colored earth tumbled.

We both held static and watched and listened to the frozen rubble as it plunged downward. It was an intimidating sight, an intimidating sound. Scary!

Then, it was quiet, except for the gusting wind and our labored breathing. We watched a tiny puff of snow powder—way down below—as one of the falling rocks struck a piece of snow-covered scrub brush. It was awesome; it was wild!

"I'm okay," shouted Jerry, finally breaking the silence, but the sound of his voice was different. It held respect, reverence. His voice had aged ten years in ten seconds.

We were both growing up fast. We were learning from a very stern mentor!

Jerry had one ice-axed hand dug in, the other was buried in snow, hopefully hooked to a handhold. One leg was stuck knee-deep into the side wall, while his other leg and boot hung in mid-air, and his ball crampon was hanging by one strap!

"Jerry!" I yelled. "You're about to lose your crampon! Pull your leg in slowly, you hear?" I had all the rope slack taken in.

"Okay, okay," he shouted, his voice sounding normal. "I hear you, I'm okay."

Slowly—very slowly—Jerry pulled his leg in, and with his non-axed hand finally freed from the snow—but still holding on to the ice ax with the other—he was able to reach back and salvage the crampon. He reattached the spike and reestablished his lock-in point. He was stabilized; he was okay!

I sighed. I was strained, fatigued. The sky was getting darker, the wind heavier. It was cold! As I pull-tightened my gloves, I noticed my fingertips poking out the end of my non-ax hand. "My gawd!" I mumbled. "In such a short time."

The rush of physical exertion and the intense concentration had dulled my mind. Was I cold, or was I not? I had to know that I was cold! If I—or Jerry—were to lose that ability, well, we may well lose it all.

It was time to move, but my bare fingers were sticking out of my glove! From scratching and digging, like a snow leopard searching for a bone, I had worn through my glove! Damn the cold, they were new gloves!

We hit the sixty foot mark and kept going, switching back-and-forth in our established routine. We no longer had any side support; we were in the middle!

Gradually, very gradually, our situation began to change. Instead of looking back toward where we came from, we started bearing on the direction we were heading. The far edge was actually getting closer!

Easy now, one step at a time. *Thud! Thud! Whack! Whack!*

We passed the half-way mark, we were pushing for the far edge.

Hot dog! I thought. My breathing was noisy and my balaclava was wet with ice from my breath. My brain was noisy. *No, no, it's the wind, no, the silence, the quiet! No, no! Dummy, how can it be quiet with the wind blowing ninety miles an hour? Pay attention, pay attention to what you're doing!*

I turned to look back at Jerry. "Okay, Jer? Can you hear me?" I shouted over the wind.

He waved back.

"Okay," I shouted! "I'm locking in, move it up, one more time!"

I had actually reached a point where I could stand with relative ease, and I had a solid chunk of black rock, at an angle, right before me that I could hang on to.

I began pulling the rope in, Jerry was at the end. "Come on, Jer," I yelled. "We got it! We got it!"

The wind was no longer gusting, it was blowing non-stop! The deep-purpled sky was as unforgiving as the wind, and the last of any daylight was being smothered into twilight. Jerry's thermometer read five below, and the windchill factor had driven the mercury well into the minus side.

The 13,000 foot lower crest came into view. We were practically level with it!

"My gawd!" Jerry gasped, catching his breath and looking ahead. "Can you believe that?!"

I almost laughed in relief. "We've almost got it, Jer." My voice cracked. "It's just ahead!"

We didn't waste any time. We picked up the pace. We were doing it! We were going to make it!

During the intensity of the previous hour, I almost didn't notice the wind and cold, but as the physical demands of The Wall subsided somewhat, the elements returned to remind me—us—that without a doubt, the force was omnipresent. The wind was cutting, the cold, brutally frigid!

"Come on, Jer, we're makin' it," I said, in almost a whisper. I wanted to reassure myself of the same fact. I, too, wanted to hear it.

And isn't it remarkable? I thought to myself. *When under stress, I hadn't felt the cold. How extraordinary. If I—or we—had crashed down that chute, would we have felt the horror? Do mice or other rodents feel anything at all, just before the strike of a talon? Do hawks and eagles and serpents hypnotize? Do we scare ourselves into oblivion? Does the adrenaline rush anesthetize? Is it the altitude, the changing of the tide, the full moon, the cold, fatigue, or the other presence?*

There were no guardians, but there surely must be angels.

As we finally made our way across that last stretch of treacherous yardage, we found ourselves on the opposite side of the ice chute. We were then clearly in sight of the 13,000 foot lower level as well as a parapet of frozen snow and ice just below it. It was as if we were invading a castle high up in the sky, and the parapet—like the moat—was put in place to repel intruders. But Jerry and I had a superior force. We would take the castle!

There was no fanfare as we finally slugged our way through the deepest snow. As we kicked and chopped our way through the parapet, a mighty west to east wind blew the loosened chunks of white stuff back over the cliff and down toward the ice chute. Oh, those poor souls who might be behind us. Of course, there was no one else.

The cold wind was so bitter and strong that Jerry and I just barely acknowledged that we, at last, had reached that point.

Yes, we had done The Crossing. We were at 13,000 feet and freezing!

Once we cleared that final lip of snow and ice, we were greeted with a piece of good news along with a little bit of the bad. The good? There was no appreciable amounts of snow along the main ridge. It had literally been blown away, over the top—as we saw, firsthand—into pseudo snowflakes that filtered their way down onto the east-sloped ice chute. The bad? We had glare ice!

Once we broke clear onto the 13,000 foot ledge, we clanked across what appeared to be sheets of clean glass; it was dangerously slick, hard-glazed ice!

My first cramponed step onto that remote, enameled surface resulted in my slipping and falling down. My pack took the brunt of the fall. Jerry helped me up, wrist-to-wrist, and we said nothing as we tried to cover our faces against the wind.

The sun was gone for the day and the deepest purple had settled in; it was the most awesome color. It seemed as if we were encased in a giant ice cube and we were looking out through the translucent wall at an eerie light being played upon us by some mystical entity. It simply did not feel like earth, it was truly supernatural.

We continued on our journey. The open plateau-like mesa was easier for travel. It was broad and relatively flat, and the large, angular rocks that were scattered about were like monuments, like statues, very cold statues.

The ground-ice dissipated, and because of our freezing hands and because our ice axes were metal, we soon reattached them to our packs. We could then, at least, move our hands and arms much more freely.

We moved at an angle, leaning to one side to counter the brutally frigid wind. Even though we had all of our clothing on our bodies, it was no appreciable match against the sub-zero onslaught.

We could not stop! Not under those conditions! We knew there was a shelter ahead; it was the only rational reason for being where we were. As it was, it was just plain suicide to be in that environment without Arctic-tested equipment, but that's the way it goes.

Only days before, we had cooked while trekking across the desert badlands; we had even questioned the possibility of ditching some of our extra clothing, but that's an old story. No, we had carried everything we thought we'd need.

Water? Yeah, we had water all right—frozen water!

I suddenly felt thirsty, and hungry, and tired, and cold.

We'd been through this before, too many times.

There was no glamour to our kind of life. We weren't on TV being noticed and watched by the millions. No, we did this kind of thing for ourselves, at a much more esoteric and soul-searching depth. To me—to Jerry—it was what men were meant to do, it goes way back. Some men are naturally drawn to their past. Why didn't *all* men hear the same call?

Have the younger generations lost their pioneering spirit, their will to regain a past? Their right to their own rite of passage? Do they not want to see and understand where they've come from? Is there a work ethic that's slowly eroding away?

After all, generations before us lived hardy lives: no automobiles, no telephones, no plumbing, no electricity, none of the plushness that we know today.

It seems the easier it becomes, the more they—the multitude—will demand. Not work for, but demand! The greedier they become, the less they appreciate.

Come. Travel with Jerry and me. You'd be thankful for a roof over your weary head. Any roof, any cave! Any shelter from the wind or hot sun. You'd appreciate a warm fire, you'd appreciate even your flashlight! It's so simple.

In the darkness, we trudged across the barren wasteland. I tried to turn my face toward the windward side, to catch a glimpse of the ghostly pinnacles that jutted up against the western horizon. Off to my right, I wanted to be awed by the severity of the drop-off; we were at the top of a straight-down precipice that drifted into infinity. With relative ease I could look east, along with the wind that practically took us to flight.

We kept on. I was in the lead. I suddenly began to feel the altitude as my head began to ache slightly. I knew the altitude would be hurting Jerry, and I looked back to see him moving zombie-like across the starched ridge. It was eerie. He looked chimeric as he moved in his own deliberate fashion.

I, too, must've looked strangely out of place, but who would know or care? Who would understand? How to explain such an experience?

I flashed back to Jerry and The Crossing, how the pivot man had held his own when The Wall had tried its best to shake him loose. I was concerned as to how he'd work it out and get out of it all, but Jerry had done well. I expected as much. Yo, partner!

I looked down at my boots and the rocks around me. I thought about how I'd looked downward a million times to watch pieces of earth go by, never to witness the same step again. I kept staring.

I could no longer see or feel the beauty of such a place—hadn't been able to for years. I had come to envy the uninitiated, who could still sense the sights and sounds of the mountains, the desert, the prairie, and the sea—people who could still experience the aroma of such noble places. Me, I could find no solace.

I didn't begrudge the fact that years had slipped by, years of learning by trial and error. It's not that my innate ability to appreciate had been lost forever. No, quite the contrary. It's just that my perspective had changed. I had simply seen enough wild. I could see it for what it truly was: raw, unsophisticated, and unsympathetic, like the earth itself. It was scree, talus, sand, and clay; it was wet, dry, chopped and smooth! It would rarely lend itself to a level piece of real estate. No, it would dip, and then drop away and become rough-hewn like an old sawbuck.

Rocks were no longer graceful shapes and shades of line and form, but ragged pieces of molten stuff that could only abuse and punish.

The sun only scorched and burned and reminded one of hell on earth; the snow and cold would take the opposite extreme and make one wish for the same hell that had just polarized the opposite sense. It was so much of the same—those places called Death Valley and Whitney.

There is an intensity to life that is spawned by the deprivation of the most basic of needs: to be cooled, warmed, fed, and slake one's thirst, all batted about within a given span of time.

And from the past, the dead burro had lain at my feet. Each night the carcass had been a meeting place, a place of feast. The red meat would glow against the snow, and the drag marks would indicate that there had been a challenge.

So it was with Jerry and I, a challenge; we were facing the reality of Mother Nature point blank—on her terms! This wasn't a vicarious secondhand episode. No, we were confronting the day-to-day obstacles head on! How many times over the years have tales of survival been lost from those who never made it?

"Yo, Jerry!" I turned and yelled at the purple-hued silhouette. "Yo, Jerry!" I called again. I could barely see him; he was moving, moving.

The wind was vicious! I doubted whether or not Jerry could even hear me but it made me feel better to yell, to break the pace, the monotony. I had to know I was still there, but it was difficult! "No!" I argued. "Getting easier."

I wanted to shut down. I moved by reflex only; I was on auto pilot, I didn't want to care anymore. I was like a robot, I was moving across the moon, a frozen moon that was barren and hostile to life. Why such a creation? Why create a place so devoid of mercy? Such savagery; my fingers were numb and fragile; my feet and toes were unnerved, as if they'd been pumped full of Novocain®.

I had to yell: "Yo! Jerry! Hang in there! We're getting there."

I squinted through my fatigued and wind-blurred eyes. "Where's the silhouette?" I murmured. "Where's the square, the straight-line?" I was looking toward the north, not at Jerry.

I continued to shuffle; I didn't want to turn a cold ankle that was devoid of feeling. I had to scrape the ground with my boot, there had to be an impulse!

I squinted again. I stopped. I strained to see through the night. "Shit. Oh dear! Looks like a roofline! It's straight! *It is* straight!" I pulled my hands up to my face and forced my eyes to work. I started moving, faster, faster!

I broke into a trot, and my pack banged and clanged against me. I stumbled and caught myself. I turned and ran sideways into the wind. I turned in the other direction so I could hear myself yell for Jerry again.

"Jerry! Jerry! Jerry! It's the hut! It's up ahead!"

I ran faster, stumbled again, and corrected myself. I kept going, yelling all the while like a crazy man.

"We're on top, Jerry! We're here! We're here!"

It was there! The hut, the stone hut! We were on top! We would have shelter!

I moved as if I were in slow motion. I reached out into the night—trying to breach the last remaining distance. Instantly, I thought of angels. *She* had led the way. The whole wild scenario transformed into a once-in-a-lifetime experience, and my brain was trying to calculate time and space. I could visualize Jerry and me inside the stone enclosure. The justification for our existence—the purpose of what we had attempted—was within our grasp.

Running cleared my head!

The stone hut was there! It was real! I could see it! I wasn't imagining, and the angel just as suddenly disappeared.

I slowed my pace to a walk, slower and slower. I came to a halt. I stared. I just stared. Then, I reached out and touched the door—and felt the stone.

We had made it!

My mind was cluttered.

There must be unclaimed powers deep within us, as well as beyond. At what point do you begin to cherish that life—life as a human being—that is much more than flesh and bone? When do you become so grateful for that life, that you long to kneel and kiss the earth that begat you?

It brought you in; it can take you out!

That parable would be forever imprinted on my humble mind.

I turned to greet Jerry as he lumbered up, like an astronaut taking his first step—or his last—before entering the Mother Ship. He looked stiff and awkward—the relentless cold had beaten us both, badly. We high-fived and then hugged as best we could considering the bulkiness of our packs and our gear.

We didn't speak. We didn't have to.

I stepped back so we could see each others' grins as they crackled across our weathered faces like variegated streaks on worn leather. We resembled kids eating cookies that had just been snatched from a secret hiding place, and those cookies were chocolate—dark colored—like our skin!

Yes, we had reached our destination. There were no words to describe the final act. We had made it up a mountain that thousands had before—easily. It would have been a cakewalk, though not the way Jerry and I did it.

Up a mountain where the throngs are usually in cut-off shorts and T-shirts, a mountain where weather can turn, in minutes, and where there will be those who won't take heed, and thus, will never return.

It was a place not to be attempted by the ill-prepared; ill prepared for a wind and cold so bitter that even stones and rocks would crack. They would crack and resettle into smaller pebbles that would eventually turn to gravel and sand and be wind-swept away into the tiny crevices and fractures where it all began in the first place.

Yeah, we were there!

We owned the mountain!

From the outside and to our left, was a door that was padlocked. The door to the right, it was unlocked.

We entered, it was dark, but immediately, the wind quit beating us.

My face flushed, as if a dam had just given way and all that was behind it was suddenly set free to rush forward and engorge any space it could find. I felt fevered as my body's blood—driven deep by the cold—began to return to the surface.

Jerry and I didn't speak as we moved deftly, by feel, working the interior of the hut. It felt like a stone ledge that circumvented the lower perimeter of the roughly eight-by-ten enclosure. The stone lip was like a sitting ledge, all the way around. We scooted up to it—just to the right of the doorway—and slid out of our packs. For several minutes, we fumbled in the dark bringing out our flashlights.

We still didn't speak; the noises and sounds of such a place did it for us. The galvanized sheet metal roof banged and clanged to the mercy of the wind; a stove pipe, with rusty wire hanging down, hovered over one of the stone corners. It creaked and groaned to the same rhythm of the wind.

At the same corner, others had built a previous fire. Small pieces of charred wood—it had to have been carried up there—was scooped up into a small pile along with chunks of blackened soot and smudged remains. And would you believe it? Someone had left an unpopped popcorn basket, complete with foil.

"Good gawd! Can you fathom this. The Ritz!"

"All the comforts of home," one of us said, matter-of-factly.

"Hell, they coulda at least left fried chicken, steak, ribs, potatoes."

"Knock it off!"

"But popcorn?"

We chuckled and moved back to our packs, and to our own silence, to the rustle of cold-frozen clothing and pack material, to the smells of damp-cold rock and musty air. We zipped and unzipped our pack pockets; there was the clanking of metal and plastic against stone, the hollow sounds of water bottles and canteens, the human sighs, and mumbles and groans, especially as we tried to work our fingers that wouldn't work. It was as if they were paralyzed with cold.

"What's the thermo read?" I asked, as flashlight beams darted about like neon blinkers.

"It was minus five at the 13,000, couldn't check in between."

"Yeah, with a what, a thirty-five to forty-mile-per-hour wind? What's that in windchill?"

"Must be forty to fifty-below out there, we're right on zero in here," Jerry was beaming his light onto his thermometer.

"Damn! You'll warm it up in here with that flashlight. We'll cook!"

"What about water?" asked Jerry.

"Snow, man, suck ice, literally! We gotta melt some!"

We continued with our packs.

"By the way, do we have the evening off?"

We laughed, finally. All of our rustling stopped. The wind continued, and Jerry and I stared at each other under the dim glow of flashlights.

"Well." Jerry shrugged his shoulders. "Here we are, we made it."

I smiled and kind of chuckled, and felt like sitting, but not on cold stone! I continued standing, so did Jerry.

"It's just now starting to hit," I said almost mechanically. "Peaceful, like heaven? Can't believe we're here."

I extended my hand.

"Yo partner! We did it!" We high-fived, and that's all the celebration there was. We were numb with unreality.

We both knew it sure as hell wasn't over with. Even though we had a substantial shelter, we'd soon feel the new cold as our bodies would readapt. We knew it was going to be a long night, we weren't celebrating. That would come weeks later, maybe months, maybe years.

"Its gonna be a long night, man," said Jerry. "And yer gear's not worth a crap!" He laughed. "That paper bag of yours."

"Ah, come on now. It'll be okay. I might get a little chilly, but it'll hold. I'll be here come morning."

And Jerry's cup fell on the stone floor.

"That's hell on hardware," I muttered as I still unpacked. "I drop my cup like that and it'd disappear."

"How long you had that thing?"

"You remember Custer?"

We laughed.

"Whatever the rules."

The sound of my frying pan against the stone ledge was one of familiarity. How many times have I heard that same sound? I would think about that. All the sounds, the blurred lights, the smells, the sense of cold, *and* hot! All were a gauge of a lifetime.

I flexed my fingers in hopes of drawing up warmer blood for their circulation; as it was, they were like hardened stubs that had no feeling, there was no muscle control. For the life of me, I couldn't properly grip my zipper pulls or force buttons through their respective holes.

My hands would only bend at the wrist, which, it turn, would press my fingers together to create a grip between a finger, or two, and my thumb. I wondered if that was the way it was for stroke victims.

I worried about frostbite. Yes, I'd had it happen before: finger tips, ear lobes, nose tip, toes! But at that particular moment, my feet felt fine. Cold yes! Frozen, hopefully not!

It was almost impossible to undo my boot strings, as they—the laces—were totally frozen into a tangled ball. But with time, and with the aid of the dull side of my knife blade, I finally undid them. Briefly, the laces resembled dark colored icicles that you'd hang on the tree at Christmas time.

It was the same situation for my boot insoles; they were frozen to the inside boot bottoms. I tore the first one in half trying to remove it. Too brittle, too cold! The accumulated moisture in my boots would just have to evaporate on its own.

I strung my rope across the ceiling for a clothesline; my funny-looking socks looked like cardboard flags. They were halfway flexible when I first took them off—to change into drier ones—but the damp, worn socks, froze even more so, as they lay crumpled at my feet.

Our water bottle lids were frozen tight. Jerry and I took turns inspecting each others' noses and ear lobes for whitish blotches—frostbite! We checked our own feet: numbed toes, but otherwise, okay, it was mainly our hands.

Finally, feeling returned, and within an hour or so, the hut temperature had risen to a mighty twelve degrees!

We busied ourselves with dinner. First though, was the melting of ice for water—for drink and for a rice dinner. The Peak-1 performed flawlessly, and it helped in warming our fingers, and mentally, we wanted to believe that that little stove was actually warming up the hut. Fat chance. We only had so much fuel and the snow water had the scorched taste of Black Mountain Whiskey. The rice, along with pieces of cheese and cocoa with milk, added to our rising spirits, but the temperature never did get above the twelve-degree mark, and the wind kept howling and banging things around. Then we went outside, one at a time, to urinate, and we each came back in, half-frozen, to swap dumb tales about our steaming urine, and how our urine froze as soon as it struck rock. How we had to stand, and brace ourselves, against the wind, backside, so as not to spray ourselves. How I walked around to the reverse side—the leeward side—of the shelter, and almost fell over when I moved into the minus wind pocket.

We joked about how we peed in fast circles so as not to become frozen to our own stream. "Oh yeah! To freeze an arc!"

We put bowel movements on hold, literally, at least until morning—if we'd survive that long!—for fear of freezing ourselves to the ground. "Oh yeah!"

We termed it: kickin' the stool! "Oh yeaaah!"

We laughed and ate and jumped around like new members to a polar club, anything to stem the cold, never sitting, moving around all the while.

Then we had our party, we had the popcorn. Even the burnt stuff was delicious.

The night grew older, and fatigue began to manifest itself; we drank our lukewarm water. As the cold became colder, and the harassing wind grew louder and louder, it was apparent that we would eventually have to settle in for the night and crawl into sleeping bags that we hoped would offer enough warmth.

The temperature snapped back to ten degrees!

We went to push-ups, it went up to twelve degrees!

We stopped, down to ten!

We ran in place, up to twelve!

We stopped, down to ten, nine degrees!

"Screw this!" One of us finally said. "It's a race! We've got to stop! We're fatigued. We're wiped out! We're operating on high!"

How true that was. Even though our situation was edgy, we both felt a supreme high; the kind of high that's spurred on by accomplishment, the inner satisfaction that's the result of a mission completed. We had followed a quest. We felt immortal, but at the same time, it didn't mean we'd become complacent. Quite the contrary.

We knew we weren't out of the woods, so to speak. We'd still take heed, we still had to get down off that mountain, and for reality's sake, we kept peeking outside to check on the sky for clouds.

We were cautious, leery. The wind that had been buffeting us, probably was the result of a low pressure system that had just passed, but what if it's the forerunner of a new, second storm? What if it clouded up and dumped a ton of snow on us? What then?

We were high, all right, but reservedly so. We weren't fools; we didn't need surprises.

We had already figured we could get the tent up inside the enclosure; that was next on the agenda.

The first space blanket would go on the ground—against the stone floor—followed by the tent itself. The second space blanket would be laid out, inside, followed by our pads and bags.

We kept our thermals on along with our heaviest and driest socks. Our hooded over-shirts and balaclavas were included, along with watch caps, and yes, gloves.

We would lie in opposite directions; we crawled in.

"Hey, man, when's the last time you washed your feet? There's smoke comin' outta the bottom of your bag!"

"Not smoke, my man, fumes!"

"Oh yeah, big time!"

"Seriously, like perfume."

"'Member those blondes out there on the Saline Valley?"

"Oh yeah, oh yeah."

And we talked about the night in the Saline Valley, the greatest. But that night, there in the stone hut, that was the payoff. We had actually made it.

We slept, at least for a while.

"Yo, Jer!" I started laughing.

"Don't tell me," came the muffled reply.

Suddenly, it all became very funny, probably a combination of altitude, fatigue, and the elation of accomplishment. I—we—were unraveling. Even being cold was suddenly funny.

"Ya know that bag I got?" I quipped.

"I knew it!" said Jerry.

"How much extra clothes you got?"

"Ha! I knew it! You're freezing!"

"Yes, my good man. I'm freezing my ass off!"

Jerry rummaged around in the dark at his end of the tent. Suddenly, his jacket hit me square in the chest, just as I sat up.

"Thanks, partner, appreciate it."

"Didn't need it, just my pillow."

"Thanks again, anyway. I've already got my legs and feet stuck in the arms of my own jacket, it's my hips and shoulders. Friggin' cold's comin' up from the ground. Thanks!"

Another hour passed.

"Yo, Jer, you asleep?"

"I really am, but go ahead."

"I don't want to startle you, but I'm gettin' up and doin' push-ups."

"Where you goin', outside?"

"Oh yeah, sure!" I crawled out of the tent. Even inside the hut, it felt bitterly cold, but it felt good to at least move around. But, there was no room outside the tent, and the ledge was too narrow.

So, back into the tent I went.

"Yo, my good man. I don't mean to startle you, but I'll be doing push-ups *in* the tent. Okay?"

"Roger-dodger," sing-songed Jerry.

"Partner, good sport!" I proceeded to do push-ups.

I rested.

"Jer! I really didn't need your jacket, just testing."

"Oh shit!" exclaimed Jerry. "You are freezin' your ass off!"

I chuckled.

I crawled back into my bag. "If we can just get past midnight," I muttered, "it'll give us the last day, the last day."

I pursed my chapped lips, and inspected them with my tongue. I pulled off my worn-fingered right glove and scratched my head and stroked my beard. I massaged my ear lobes. Then, I flexed my hands and fingers, then my feet and toes. All were okay. "I'll be in one piece for the last day." I was still muttering to myself. "Just don't freeze, no siree, don't dare freeze; give us the last day."

I wondered what my kids were doing; I smelled perfume, there was a wisp of blond hair.

I guess I slept.

CHAPTER 14

DAY 14

Mt. Whitney

Brief moments of time seemed like hours as the night departed into eternity. Actual hours seemed to ignore the fact that—just maybe—there would be daylight once again as the wind, still battered away fiercely, had more or less lullabied us all through the hectic night in its own convulsive and moronic way. The gale-force gusts would roar down upon the hut, bang away, then grow silent for brief moments, only to return in full fury from a new direction. It reminded me of the katabatic winds of the Superstitions of Arizona where the wild devil gusts would perform in the same bizarre fashion.

The winds showed no indication of abating as a yellowish hue began to finally manifest itself across the eastern portion of the sky. Gradually, the yellow-orange light began to filter into the interior of the stone enclosure, even permeating through the tent fabric itself. A brilliant sun was making its debut; the night was finally over.

Jerry awoke with a start. He was surprised to see me already awake and sitting, upright, in my bag.

"How's it going?" I asked, solemnly. "Sun's comin' up. We're on top of the world."

"Well, I just pinched myself," said Jerry. "I guess we're alive, huh?"

"You bet, man! You ought to take a look out that east window. We're probably catchin' the sun before anybody else."

"No wonder," said Jerry, fully awake, and excited. "We're on the highest point in the country. What are we, 14,000-and-something?"

"14,395, or '495. I think. I'm not sure which. I've seen different figures."

"What are you doing?" asked Jerry, as he caught a glimpse of my note pad.

"Just loggin' us in. How's this sound?" I read:

"Successfully reached the summit of Mt. Whitney approximately 8 pm, October 26th, '89...the event marked a unique, unprecedented 125-mile, first attempt, along a 280-degree compass course, cross-country, from Badwater, Death Valley to the summit of Whitney...the entire trek took 14 days; the two men left Badwater, October 14th, '89... the men endured countless hardships: high temperatures of 110 degrees in Death Valley, to subzero conditions on Mt. Whitney; lack of water, isolated conditions; the crossing of some of the most hostile and treacherous land in the world... the trek included the Panamint Range, the Slate, the Argus, the Inyo Range, and finally, the Sierra...."

"I like it, the way it was, the way it is. You wrote that this morning?" Jerry asked.

"Yeah, got up early. Push-ups, ya know."

Jerry laid back pulling a sock—dubbed as a scarf—up tight around his neck. "Damn, it's cold! Whew-eee! Maybe I could run in place in my bag!"

"That'd be a trick all right," I replied. "By the way, your thermometer still reads 12 degrees, We must really be insulating this place."

"Wonder what it'd be like without the wind," said Jerry.

"You can only get so cold," I continued. "And there's not a cloud in the sky, just windy as hell."

"At least we'll be able to see our way down. Can you believe it? We're going down, goin' home!" Jerry was reversing his flashlight batteries.

There was a tacit euphoria within ourselves, a privacy, and regardless of the raw environment, we were elated about where we were and about what we had accomplished. We could see it, feel it, and hear it from one to the other. It was in the tone of our voices; the tenseness was gone, there was the absence of urgency, and for some undefined, visual reason, we could see it in each other's faces. You could read it. We were going out; it was our last day.

We weren't really cognizant of the cold or the wind, nor was there any immediate feeling, or fear, of re-tracking the ice chute. After all, we'd cut a damned good trail! And there was sunshine; we'd be okay, and we believed that.

But, supposing, during the night, a storm had blown in; supposing it was snowing outside—hard! A blizzard!

We thought about that, too, privately. We knew what could've been. Yeah, the rest of the story.

No, no celebrating. We'd wait. We still had time. We still had to get all the way down.

As it was, we were overdue. We really didn't know by how much, nor did we really care. There were others who did, but not us. We were on a different emotional level, and it is peculiar how that phenomenon manifests itself. One man could be locked away in isolation, and could go crazy with time. Another could be fully involved with a frantic race against the same time, but it would not be the same. One could drowse in an easy chair in front of the fireplace, it could be storming outside, but warm and cozy on the inside. Another being could be wallowing in a trench half-full of cold mud, during the same storm. Time would suddenly take on a totally different connotation; one would see the storm, the other, the sunshine.

Obviously, Jerry and I lived and breathed every finite detail of our ordeal. Others could think about it. We could too—but only briefly—before carrying on with our day-to-day lives. And that's okay. We all do the same, it's human nature.

Yes, Jerry and I were overdue.

Yes, my mind was muddled.

And yes, even on that last morning, we really did feel the cold!

The wind kept blowing, but we listened in our own silence.

Suddenly, I felt as though I didn't want to go back. I wanted to stay high. I wanted to stay above it all. We could've looked, intimately, at the tiny rocks and fissures, the grains of sand. They would've been oblivious to all others things too. So it was with Jerry and I, and I wouldn't be able to explain that to anybody else. Not for awhile anyway.

I mumbled, "Hey Lee, where you been? Camping?"

I answered myself, "Oh yeah, sure."

And again, I muttered under my breath, "Asshole! You'd never understand, never!"

Like combat. Don't try and explain, don't even try!

And to those on the flatland, the civilized, I continued, "Keep complaining about your cars and clothes and having to walk half a block to the mall. Keep complaining about your leaking roofs, your overheated houses, your running water, your comfy bathrooms, and your warm showers. You people just don't realize what you have. The easier it gets for you, the more you want, the more you complain, and the deeper you get, until you totally bury yourselves in your own sea of self-pity."

I didn't seem myself. I knew what altitude could do, but there was no control. I would stay muddled, almost confused, almost numb, and I thought about a warm fire. Could I control that fire? Would I burn down the hut? *No, stupid! It's rock!*

I tucked away my journal. I ran my hand over my thermal top and across my skin-tight belly. I massaged the upper part of my thighs. "Easy fella, not much further now." I flexed my cold fingers, my toes.

We finally crawled out of our bags and bundled up with all of our clothing to store what warmth we had. We rolled our bags and stuck our heads outside the tent flap to marvel at the sunshine that peeked through the tiny east window that was covered with a thick plexiglass.

We struck the tent. That gave us enough room to get our packs together. Even though we had light—sunshine—the bitter cold never ceased, nor did the everlasting wind. It just wasn't going to turn us loose.

We fired up our little stove and melted ice for drinking water. We finished off the last of our cereal and powdered milk and split the last of our cheese. We'd high-pack an orange, apiece, for lunch. We had slept with our oranges to keep them from freezing. I pulled mine out to show off to Jerry.

"Look!" I said. "One of my balls froze up orange!"

"Tough shit!" returned Jerry. "I always thought you had two of 'em!"

I feigned throwing the orange at Jerry, laughing. "On second thought, I'll hold off. Either you miss it, and I wind up with a crippled orange for lunch, or you'll catch it and brag about having two orange balls! No way, man!"

That started our morning.

Last but not least—and reluctantly—I actually set up my tiny, metal tripod. I kept my gloves on, knowing full well that flesh and frozen metal don't mix. Savvy?

I screwed my Nikon® onto the top of my mini-tripod. Very slowly, and carefully, I cranked the film advance. I knew the film could snap because of the cold, but it didn't.

I fired off a couple of self-timed shots.

You should see our faces! Just look!

Going from the hut and out into the wind was like moving into a different world—a world of noisy confusion and chaos. No wonder animals are so skittish and nervous when the wind blows. No wonder they can't hear anything, except the wind! And it's not really the wind, per se, but the effects of the wind; so it was with Jerry and me.

Think about that! You're constantly on the alert simply because the wind masks every other noise that you should be aware of, all the subtleties: the sound of your boots against the ground, the sounds of rock and gravel, the sounds of your arms rubbing against fabric, and the creaks and groans of your own pack.

There are sounds that emit from running water or falling rock; the bark, yip, or growl from an animal, the screech of a hawk, your own breathing, or the sounds from another person, or persons, in distress or otherwise. Animals don't hear the critical snap of a twig or the attack-flutter of wings if everything is moving—trees, brush, weeds. The wind, and the sounds it creates, conceivably mask the slightest twinge of a stalking predator.

Likewise, humans don't hear animals when the wind blows; nobody hears anything, there is no silence!

Because of that ubiquitous wind, Jerry and I would tie our jacket hoods down tight, which, in turn, would make for even more noise; it also limited our visual line-of-sight. This was particularly true when the wind force fought against us. From behind, not quite so bad, but face-on, or sideways, it was big time noise!

So it was as we left that stone hut from atop Mt. Whitney on our fourteenth day.

There was a log book. It was in a lidded box, held down by a rock, just to the left of the front door.

We hadn't taken the time to read any of the entries; that would be for another time. Summertime, perhaps, on a medium-tempered day or night with no wind. Perhaps, with companions all decked-out in cut-off shorts, and t-shirts, maybe light jackets and day-packs, and the leisurely time to go "Oooo" and "Ahhh" at the unusual entries, such as: "Badwater to Whitney, cross-country, October, 1989."

Yeah, cool.

Jerry and I literally had our hands full signing our cold-fingered signatures to the enclosed entry. We struggled to keep the lid from blowing off, which included the clipped papers inside. Then, we slammed the lid down and replaced the rock. We high-fived.

We started down, Jerry in the lead.

He leaned and swayed with the wind's erratic oscillations. Occasionally, he'd bring his arms up, suddenly, in balance, like bird wings, to counter the heaviest wind gusts that were like barrel blasts. Jerry was once again the pivot man, hangin' ten, walkin' the dog.

There were no clouds, at all, throughout the entire sky, and we knew—almost for sure, from experience—that there would be considerably less wind as we'd move away, and down, from the crest, but that was at least a mile-and-a-half distance: the 13,000 foot ice shelf!

That was our immediate goal, and as we moved in that direction, it was slightly downgrade. It felt good. We started watching for ice, and we tried to calculate and bring into perspective—mentally, to ourselves—the sights and places we hadn't seen in the dark the night before. And as always, it's like traveling in new country, as if we'd never been there before.

In no time, the 13,000 foot lower summit was in view. We moved slower; we became cautious. Ice! And then we were there.

We crunched down behind the leeward side of the finger rock. This time, however, it was free of wind. It was shelter!

Almost immediately, without the wind buffeting us, and with the sun's rays directly upon us, the temperature felt like eighty-degrees. Of course, it wasn't, it was just our body's temperature mechanism following its natural cycle of adaptation. It was being fooled by the wind and our clothing: the greens and reds of our jacket shells that drew in the sun's power.

When we moved away from the rock shelter to stand and quickly look over the rock line to catch a glimpse of the ice chute, below, the wind gusts would then lash at us like sleet against sails.

The chute was there, all right, sinister-looking, as it lay there with its straight-down, cut-sized walls and in its own, self-created deep shadow. But like before, the chute was lower down and out of the way of the assaulting west-to-east wind.

Even the finger-rock-shelter was sufficient for only a short while as the wind began to eddy into slipstreams. The unpredictable gusts seemed to play tag all along the ridgeline as the sun rose higher.

Yes, the ice chute would be still and quiet, but there'd be no sun, it would be cold! However, being on the ridgeline was also cold. We had sun, but we also had sporadic wind. Take your pick.

Whereas the lowest point in the country—the salt bogs—had been the anus of America, the ice chute surely had to be the armpit. No two ways about it.

It was back to crampons and ice axes.

Much to our glee, as we crunched into the very top portion of the chute, we realized it wasn't going to be the problem that it had been before. It was frozen!

It was mush frozen. It was crunchy, just the right consistency, the result of the cold night and early morning.

Yes siree. We had cut a damned good trail. Our previously stomped crampon holes were like bowls molded into soft rock, but those same holes would soften as the day would grow older. The minute we worked our way over the edge, we were out of the wind.

But still, with hoods, balaclavas, and caps snugged down tight, and a newly discovered world of silence, we laid out our rope.

The sudden quietude of the moment seemed to ease the mental tension. Our temperaments changed; we relaxed a bit, but not to the point of becoming complacent or careless. The calm let us feel again. It seemed as though our thinking became clearer. "Be cool now," I mumbled to myself. *Don't screw up; don't get careless. We're too close, too close to the end. It must end our way!*

Jerry picked his way across, carefully.

"How's it over there?" I kept asking in a loud enough voice, but not really having to shout. In fact, we could communicate without having to strain to hear, nothing like the yelling and shouting of before.

We continued.

Steady now, steady, no slips, we're too close. It was comforting to hear my own voice, my own breathing.

We worked our ice axes to the downhill side of the slope, and I flashed back to my firefighting days as a kid. "All tools to the downside," our foreman, King McCall, would shout. "If you fall, damn it, throw the tools out, outta the way, downside!"

The memories flooded in: California Tools, McCleods®, Pulaskis, mattocks, axes, tamp bars, brush hooks, shovels, back pumps, and Bean Sprayers® off the back of Dodge Power Wagons®.

Jerry and I probed the downside with our axes like walking sticks, and we probably looked like old men, with canes, searching for the curb at a bus stop. My mind was suddenly flooded with memories of the past again and again, the years of trail work: G-3/black powder, cut 'n fill, decomposed granite (DG), rain-bars, star drills, and the veteran powder monks who would sit around the campfire at night digging pieces of mercury out of their hands with pocket knives.

There were the all-Mexican and all-Indian fire crews who'd Hot-Shot into the bigger campaign fires. There were prisoners from Folsom and Soledad; Wards of the State from the Youth Authority (CYA); road gangs, trail gangs, and Blister Rust gangs from the Department of Corrections (CDC); and other Hot-Shot crews from Blasinggame to Utah and Idaho.

I snapped back; Jerry was punching through. That was good. He was striking sound as the snow had packed up much tighter than before.

We played our ropes: slack 'n taut, slack 'n taut. We moved well; we felt good. We were still very much aware of the effects of altitude, and we'd literally verbalize our instructions, one to the other—and repeat them—so that we were fully aware of what the other was doing. We had to rely on one another. We were literally bringing each other out, and it'd been that way all along; it would continue that way clear to the last.

Pieces of snow would occasionally break away, and we'd stop and watch the snowballs cascade downward. When the ball would hit softer stuff, it would make a line, and the snowball would get bigger and bigger.

We'd watch those 'wall balls' spiral downward, as if watching a movie, and they'd finally streak apart like fireworks in the rocks far down below, and as we watched the mini-drama take place, we could only imagine ourselves in such a scenario: tumbling down, the same way.

"Never," I mumbled. *"Never."*

Suddenly, Jerry shouted.

"We got it! We got it!" He was close to the full sixty feet away; he picked up the pace.

"We got it!" he shouted again. His voice boomed as he turned toward my direction. Even at our distance, I could see his broad smile, and he was pulling the rope.

"Yooo!" I bellowed back. "We're on the way; we're gettin' there!"

Jerry had his arms outstretched like Sir Edmond.

He was across the ice chute, I was right behind.

Jerry was drawing in, and re-coiling the rope as he spotted for me while I moved across the last section of white crust. When we finally came together, we high-fived so vigorously we almost lost our balance. Then, like excited kids at a birthday party, we stomped and kicked and turned about in small circles, trying to make more room to stand. We were exuberant!

Without being fully aware of it, we'd been apprehensive about our return over The Chute. Sure, our focus had been narrowed to surviving the night atop Whitney, but, obviously, other concerns had manifest themselves as well. They do sneak in. We all ponder—worry—over countless details that cross our minds within a given time frame. We access such minor items as being integral parts of our daily lives, while at the same time, still concentrating on the major ones, the major obstacles.

Just completing the trek itself was major enough, while going back over the ice chute was only one of many minor problems we had confronted. Nonetheless, The Chute soon loomed up as a major concern, but then, every day had been a major concern: the bogs, the canyons, lack of water, too much snow and ice! The Chute had been just one more added concern.

We had accepted the challenge and had excelled. It was behind us, literally! It was history!

Not only did the final crossing free our minds, in that respect, but the energy that had been drawn, in way of worry, was enervating to both mind and body. When freed up, that energy was then made available for all faculties, the very ones that had been depleted in the first place. It was like turning water to wine, the strength from within.

Thus, at that point, we were mentally and physically as high as the mountain itself. We had drunk of the wine.

We pulled our hoods back to greet the additional warmth from no wind and to expose our faces—and our broad smiles—to whomever would see us: the whole world! Yeah, sure: the mice, the crickets, the ants, all the bugs. All those little guys who never get credit. Yeah, the whole world! Here's to you, yeah!

That's how we felt, Jerry and me. We had a piece of it!

Then we pulled off our balaclavas, because it was warmer, even in deep shade. We had also dropped down in elevation by a couple thousand feet, and still, no wind.

Following our own crampon tracks, finally slicing into the Brits' tracks, and by virtue of the fact that we were going downgrade, well, what can I say, it was like flying. It took no effort, and we felt like birds, big birds, full of energy, yeah, testosterone energy! A strength from within. The kind of strength that men revel in; a kind of strength that fewer and fewer men experience, strong and unshaken in a commitment, in control of a destiny from past and present lives. Yet, there was a dedicated responsibility. Yes, we were responsible for what we were doing. Become lost, injured? Who would we blame? The government?

I chuckled to myself. *Oh yeah, sue the government. What do they have to do with what I—we—do? No, no! Sue God! Oh yeah.* I smiled and looked down at the snow, and at my boot as it slushed in.

I'm almost comfortable, I thought. *I can dream about such dumb things now. Sorry God, wouldn't think of it!*

Then we hit ice. Rock-hard ice! It was near the bottom of the snowfield. Suddenly, we pulled ourselves back—mentally.

Easy now, easy.

Jerry still held the lead. While we thought we had retired our rope, for good, we suddenly drew from it one more time. It was back to work as before, and it became colder as we slowed down and gingerly worked our way over the lower snowpack.

The crusty white stuff had gone from crunchy to solid as we slowed our pace even more. We began kicking our way across the zigzagged slope like miniature snowmaking machines in high gear, our rope lying slack, just in case.

Just below the snowfield were the rocks where we first met the Brits, the ones who, well, you know the story.

And then the rocks were there! Right in front of us!

Without fanfare, we undid our crampons and laid aside our ice axes. They were put back in place, snubbed to our packs, along with rope and all the other stuff that was slung to our backsides.

We worked our way back over to the start—the bottom—of the switchbacks. The metal poles and cable were still there just as we had seen them before, frozen tight in their white base.

Then there was mud, then dirt, then a twinge of dust.

We finally pulled off our caps. It was warmer, still.

Trail Camp was next. We went straight through and kept going. Next, it was Outpost Meadows. We stopped. It was cold again under the canopy of the first and last of the timber. There was sunshine, but the warmth was dependant on the time of day, and the direction you might be heading.

Finally, it was midday, time for our orange balls.

We moved to a sun rock, ate our oranges, and almost fell asleep. We were starting to unravel.

Without warning, all of the energy we had conjured up just hours before, all the steam and angst of coming down was suddenly being drained away like oxygen from a leaking bottle.

I looked over at Jerry and marveled. A hell of a partner! He could do a toe dance on a knife point, I swear. But he was tired.

I nodded off; I snapped back. "Time to go," I slurred, as I stuffed my orange peels into my pocket. "My orange ball is no more, gotta get more."

Jerry rose. He sighed, but didn't speak. He was tired.

I chuckled and mumbled to myself, "Who isn't; we're hammered, but we made it."

We continued downward and it got warmer and warmer. Our perspective of what was warm or cold had been thoroughly skewed by what we had endured. To us, it might feel warm; others would be cold, very cold!

So it was, near the end of the afternoon, when we suddenly came upon some day-hikers. They were admiring the ice-covered ponds near one of the lower meadows. They were bundled up like Eskimos, and, from a distance, they looked like big giant rabbits frolicking in the woods as they *Oooo'd* and *Ahhh'd* at the sights.

Jerry and I surprised the small group as we approached. We slowed our pace when we noticed they had stopped their antics and were staring at us.

One young girl, bolder than the others, approached, but held up, suddenly, as she got closer. She sensed that Jerry and I were not of the ordinary.

We stopped. Then, I stepped out ahead of Jerry to give myself some room. I was close enough, at that point, to notice a change of expression on the girl's face.

She looked surprised; she spoke.

"My, it's cold today, isn't it?"

I stopped and looked at her, but didn't answer.

She spoke again, "Is there a toilet around?"

For a split second, I felt like an eagle, and my stare must've been like a laser. Again, for that split second, I almost relished the fact that I was intimidating her.

"Ma'am," I said in my most manly voice—and the more frail and out-of-place she looked, the more manly I felt—"if you have to go, then go!" and I nodded to the left, to the open land.

"Oh," she replied, shyly, while at the same time bringing mittened fingertips up to her mouth, as if in shock. "Oh, oh, okay." She forced up a smile and took a step backward.

That girl, along with her companions, knew for sure that they had just met men from another planet. Yes, indeed.

Jerry and I moved on. When we were out of sight from the day'ers, we began to chuckle and snicker. It had been fun, bless 'em, but they were pukes! Even though, she was a real cutie.

The term "puke" is not to be taken as a derogatory remark. It's just that she was so pale and clean looking, and she smelled good. Damn! She looked good! She wasn't weathered and beat-up looking; her clothes were fresh and new, not worn and tattered and soiled with mud and dirt; fourteen-day-old crud.

It suddenly dawned on me just how out of place *we* really were, but then, I've known that for years. How difficult it was to return from the outer world. To return to civilized surroundings and pretend you're like everyone else, when in fact, you're not.

It's like the combat veteran. You are simply not compatible with the life you once came from. Something changes, something just doesn't fit anymore. You hold to that for the rest of your life.

The mountains and desert do the same thing. You leave something there and bring something back in return. It becomes a rite of passage! *"...you've stolen away your mother's key,"* as Robert Bly would say.

Where's the discipline, the character, the esteem? It comes from struggle! It comes from seeing and experiencing the underbelly of life. It comes from direction!

The mountains can teach you; the isolation and deadly environment of the desert can teach you. There is no left or right, you narrow through the middle. There are no second chances. We continued on, it was getting toward dusk.

And then we saw it.
Lights!

It was Whitney Portal, just below.

There were lights.

Yes, headlights!

There were people there. We could hear them.

And we suddenly found ourselves at the top of the wooden planking that was the beginning of the trail to the top of Whitney, from the Portal.

The lights were beamed on Jerry and me; they were headlights.

There was Doyle, with his wife, Pat. And there was Sue.

The lights were blinding, confusing. It was black of night, and it was cold to the ones waiting, but to Jerry and me, the night was tempered with warmth.

There was pizza and cola and the fragrance of clean bodies and fresh clothing. There was the scent of perfume and, yes, once again, there were wisps of blond hair.

There had been others waiting as well, but nobody really knew when, or how—or *even*, if—Jerry and I were coming down as there'd been no sign of us since we ventured away from the Portal, just days prior.

Then, the storm that had moved in and left many with uneasy doubts. Nobody knew anything.

People can't wait forever, especially into the night, the cold night.

As the evening wore on, Jerry and I would learn that other climbers had watched us through binoculars from far below as we made our final crossing just below the 13,000 foot level. From that point on, it was anybody's guess.

And there was more pizza and cola and perfume and flash pops from cameras.

Terra firma!

Epilogue

As the months and years would pass on, there would be other stories, as well. Not just about Jerry and me, no, but about others; others who wouldn't fare as well, they'd not make it, they'd not survive!

Why do some perish, while others live on? Must there be losers for there to be winners? Do some adhere more fervently to a discipline than others? Do some listen more intently? Listen to the wind, the earth? Do some follow the clouds and the stars as if they were spirits? Is there a destiny?

For the rest of us, is there a God?

Maybe there are no guardians as we know them, but could there be angels?

I ask again: if there are angels, why do others perish? Why would a man die trying to cross the bogs in Death Valley the year after Jerry and I crossed? Why would a man die, later on, at the Whitney hut because of a lightning strike? Why would a jet aircraft fail and crash and cause the death of the pilot? The crash would take place along a mid-point of our desert crossing. Why would others lose their lives at the very ice chute where Jerry and I had crossed?

There would also be Reney, who would die, suddenly, after seven days in the Panamints. I would be proud of her and miss her, dearly, as I would be one of the remaining few to share with her the experience of a truly remote wilderness.

What about my mother, my stepmother, my father, and, finally, my sister? Why did they have to leave? I ask again: is there an angel?

Yes and no: angels of mercy, I suppose.

But could there not be others, as well? Ones who protect, ones who show the way?

Are there unknown entities that roam the mountains and desert? Who or what is it that moves so deftly in the night, or in the dark of day?

I'll always admit to the feeling of another presence as Jerry and I trekked across such a forbidden land, and I've felt and experienced the same phenomenon when trekking by myself.

But with Jerry and I especially, someone, or something must've surely been watching over us as we traversed such wild canyons. What about the bogs? Why did we make it across, and someone else, not? What about the ice chute? Who really led the way across and on to the top of Whitney? Who's been watching all these years?

"Could there really be an angel? I asked myself as I leaned back against the roughened log that finally gave me rest. I let my eyes close, and I drifted off momentarily as the cool night air rolled over me like a veil.

I opened my eyes, slightly, and leaned forward. I watched Jerry as he moved in and out of the glaring lights. I watched Doyle in his excitement about it being over with. And Pat—Doyle's wife—would drift in and out of the shadows, while

Sue moved left, then right, with her camera, her blondish hair backlighted against her olive-colored jacket.

Beyond, it was dark. The headlights further transformed the dark into pitch black. Then, there was no beyond. It was just empty. Yet, I knew 'She' must be out there. I wanted to believe that she was just waiting to make sure all was well before going her way, until next time.

There was harmony. I was elated, and it seemed as though I was floating on air, the sky, and I could've walked back into the darkness, back onto the mountain, and beyond, to the eventual desert. I would not have felt fear, for I knew she would've been there.

I dozed off again. There was a sudden dream. It was calming, peaceful. Yes, indeed, there must have been an angel.

About the Author

Lee Bergthold has spent the past 50 years trekking across remote regions of the desert and mountain Southwest United States. He travels solo, and with hand-picked, pre-trained companions who specialize in survival techniques. The author still maintains a rigorous schedule of 80 to 100 days a year in the backcountry, roaming isolated regions where few others dare tread: Northern Nevada to the Mexican border; Utah to the Sierra Nevadas...all points between. Bergthold's forays range from 10 days to 35 days, specifically when exploring Donner Party migration routes.

Bergthold is authoring three other books: <u>To Walk Away From Battle Mountain</u>; <u>The Night of the Triangle</u>; and <u>The Hastings Cutoff</u>.

Bergthold is a former Marine (Korean War) and is professor of Photography/Photojournalism at Antelope Valley College, where he also conducts survival seminars.

Printed in the USA
CPSIA information can be obtained
at www.ICGtesting.com
LVHW011216280124
770159LV00009B/1015